HAVE
SEX
LIKE YOU
JUST
MET...

HAVE SEX LIKE YOU JUST MET...

No Matter How Long You've Been Together

EVERY Girl's Guide TO A *Sexy & Satisfying* RELATIONSHIP

JOSELIN LINDER & ELENA DONOVAN MAUER

Avon, Massachusetts

Published by
Adams Media, a division of F+W Media, Inc.
57 Littlefield Street, Avon, MA 02322. U.S.A.
www.adamsmedia.com

ISBN 10: 1-60550-664-8
ISBN 13: 978-1-60550-664-7

Printed in the United States of America.

J I H G F E D C B A

Library of Congress Cataloging-in-Publication Data
is available from the publisher.

This publication is designed to provide accurate and authoritative information
with regard to the subject matter covered. It is sold with the understanding that
the publisher is not engaged in rendering legal, accounting, or other professional advice. If legal advice or other expert assistance is required, the services
of a competent professional person should be sought.
    —From a *Declaration of Principles* jointly adopted by a Committee of the
American Bar Association and a Committee of Publishers and Associations

Many of the designations used by manufacturers and sellers to distinguish their
product are claimed as trademarks. Where those designations appear in this
book and Adams Media was aware of a trademark claim, the designations have
been printed with initial capital letters.

*This book is available at quantity discounts for bulk purchases.
For information, please call 1-800-289-0963.*

ACKNOWLEDGMENTS

First and foremost, we would like to thank all the women—and a few men—who shared honest, personal, wise, helpful, hilarious, embarrassing, brilliant, and graphic details from their sex lives. Whether you did it over a few bottles of wine, over the phone, by e-mail or in everyday gossip, without you, this book would not exist. And it certainly wouldn't be as relatable, funny, or useful as we think it is.

We would like to thank Molly Lyons for her endless support, advice and re-reads, not to mention a friendship we both feel very fortunate to have. We would also like to thank Meredith O'Hayre for her incredible dedication to our books and her unparalleled editing chops. We'd like to thank Jacquinn Williams for committing so much time to getting us on the radio, in bookstores, and on posters—despite the devil horns (ahem . . .). We'd like to thank Judith Steinhart for welcoming us into her home and sharing her wisdom; we're psyched to come to a "sexuali-tea." Also, thanks to Lauree Ostrofsky, Dr. Eva Altobelli, Dr. Charlie Kilpatrick, Sarah Stark, Katy Zvolerin, and Malee Ackerman for their priceless and expert advice. This book is far richer because of it.

Elena would like to thank Tony for being understanding about her weekends spent in front of a laptop and for giving her all the time she needed to write—that included cooking dinners and walking the dog so she didn't lose her train of thought. (And for offering to pause the movie when she left the room. She wasn't watching the movie. She was writing a book. But thank you.) Also, thank you to Mom and Dad for being supportive and not disowning her for writing about such not-so-good-girl stuff. To Amber who has been her biggest fan for the last, oh I don't know, fifteen years, thank you for telling her exactly why she should write this book.

Joselin would like to thank all the Tigers for so much of their time and energy devoted to encouraging her to write and keep writing. She'd like to thank her family for such resounding support—you'd think she was writing about curing cancer instead of finding G-spots. She has to thank her father for taking her and her sister into the bathroom when they were kids and teaching them all the swear words and their meanings. She is sure this somehow helped her in the writing of this book. She'd like to thank her mother for letting her trip gracelessly into a career, her sister for pretending like she's always had success, and her grandmother for preordering copies of her books no matter the topic (and passing them around the retirement community). She has to thank Aaron for tolerating a know-it-all girlfriend and sometimes even letting her think she actually knows it all. And to their dog, Dee Dee, for no longer sleeping on the bed.

Contents

CHAPTER 1

THE *SEXIFICATION* AND *DESEXIFICATION* OF RELATIONSHIPS . . . 1

TEACHING HIM . . .
AND
LETTING HIM
TEACH YOU . . . 57

HAVE **SEX** LIKE YOU **JUST** MET . . .

CHAPTER 9

UTILIZING *TRICKS* OF THE *TRADE—* THE WORLD'S *OLDEST* TRADE . . . 175

Introduction

Love, Fidelity, and Happiness

"My ex-boyfriend and I dated for almost two years, and we never had sex. For that matter, we barely made out. He also had a group of friends that I never met, and heaven forbid that we spend the entire weekend together or even one night during the week. I was just so into him that the sex part didn't bother me at first, but then when we stopped making out, that's when it became a real problem. The relationship ended and he said that I was too 'needy,' which I know I am not."

—Marie

You've picked up a book with the word "sex" written in neon pink on its cover. And, no, you're no ho. You've simply acknowledged that having a great sex life can benefit your long-term relationship —plus, it's ridiculously fun to be having great sex, or so you've heard. But where is this utopia where not only do you both work hard and have great social lives but you also have the time, energy, and wherewithal to get some toe-curling action on the side? In fact, never mind *on the side*, whoop-dee-doo about the hard work and the social life, where in God's name (or okay, maybe not *God's* name) is the fabulous S-E-X?!

Improving your sex life can be a tough thing to do. It can be awkward to talk about sex with your guy, no matter how close you two are—and it's even an embarrassing topic to bring up with your most trusted girlfriends. So that's why we wrote this book. We wanted to create an open, honest forum for discussing monogamous sex, to discover some foolproof tips for keeping it hot, no matter how long you've been together. And then to put it all out there on the big satin sheet–covered bed of your choosing.

What Is Monogamy and How Did Humans Catch It?

"Mono" is the illness that maybe you caught in the eighth grade (maybe from kissing a boy) that made you very, very, very tired. "Monotone" is the quality that describes the way the dull-as-nuts teacher spoke in *Ferris Bueller's Day Off*. Remember: "Bueller . . . Bueller . . . ?" That guy made everyone in the class tired. So what does "monogamy," another "mono-" word, really mean—is it just something that makes every long-term relationship completely, well, exhausted?

If you're a definition kind of gal, know that *Merriam-Webster* defines monogamy as "the condition or practice of having a single mate during a period of time." (We like how it's called a *condition*, like it's some disease we caught.) According to recent research, there are three types of monogamy: sexual (only doing it with one person), social (living and raising kids with one person, but doing it with others, too), and genetic (only having babies with one person—ever).

Generally, monogamy is desirable. People in our society tend to want to pair off. Love and fidelity are considered good things. Proof? You probably spent most of your life as a single gal searching for the right guy to spend quiet Sunday nights with. It was a goal—and it's been our goal, was your mother's goal and probably 95 percent of your girlfriends' goals. But it's not like there's necessarily an innate force that make us want it.

In fact, monogamy is largely unnatural. There are approximately 5,000 species of mammals on Earth, and only about 3 to 5 percent of them mate for life. (This minority includes foxes, otters, beavers, and wolves.)

Ninety percent of birds are monogamous—but many are only *socially* monogamous. They live and raise their young together, but have sex with other partners. (No, we don't know how birds have sex and don't really want to know. We're just saying.)

Ultimately, humans aren't wholly monogamous either. (Can we hear a "No duh," from the bleacher seats?) In fact, *polygamy* or the practice of marriage between more than one person still exists in many parts of the world, including Utah. We're talking as many as 80 to 85 percent of cultures accepting it, depending on which study you read. There are those that contend that in some places, such as India and China, it is merely a question of finances that keep polygamy rates as low as they are. After all, a girl's got to have her Prada shoes—two wives mean twice as much Prada shoe buying. In disease-prone regions there is often a higher rate of polygamy, which some attribute to women seeking a dude with a suitable gene pool over an excellent dancer. But women don't get to get too huffy about how unfair it seems that guys are the only ones who benefit from this practice. In one region of India, polyandry, or marriage of more than one *man* to one *woman*, is still in practice. In this case, a group of brothers share one wife to keep conflict over precious land to a minimum. But we realize that that sounds both creepy and incredibly unpleasant.

Then, of course, there are those occasional stories about polygamous sects in Texas or Florida—and TV shows like that one on HBO about three wives sharing one husband . . . and one big backyard. While it's technically illegal to practice polygamy in the United States, there are still some people out there who do it. So why be with someone who's with someone else, too? Is there any truth to the whole thing about men needing to plant a lot of seeds? The truth is, some people do see an anthropological link to what we will technically call "being a scumbag," but in fact, we believe that men can and usually do keep it in their pants—as much as women, anyway. We like monogamy because it gives us something special: a life partner—a Sunday morning cuddle-bunny, a person to check our car's oil levels, and someone from whose plate we can comfortably pilfer french fries. Bottom line? It feels right.

Monogamy as we know it has an inconclusive origin. In human history, some believe it became socially expected first in Greco-Roman times. Think about those mythological Gods—remember how they were married but always cheating on each other? Remember people getting turned into constellations, marble statues, or various species of flora and fauna as punishment? If there's such a thing as "cheating" that is punishable by de-animation, then that means there's such a thing as "monogamy" that must be the desired or sought-after behavior, right? Others think it goes back to some nomadic tribes whose leaders would teach the men of the tribe to stay monogamous for an ulterior motive: To keep the population numbers lower so the tribe could continue to easily move from place to place. Of course, religious purists contend that the practice of staying with one person is as old as the first people on the planet, Adam and Eve. Whatever you believe, monogamy is part of Western culture, no matter what Warren Jeffs has brainwashed you into believing. It doesn't matter whether you're talking marriage or a sort of "serial monogamy"— being with just one person during a given period of time, then breaking up and moving on to another *one* person. Monogamy really is our societal norm, is it not?

In our society, love and romance are important to relationships, especially marriage. Because we women are now making our own money and don't need to "marry into it," practices like arranged marriage and polygamy are in many cases obsolete.

We also think monogamy is a sign that humans have evolved. We're different from animals. Some experts believe that monogamy has only evolved in animals whose offspring benefit from both partners staying together long-term—as is the case with human children, who take a long time to mature. Some of us are in our thirties and still not sure we're fully mature.

So, perhaps it's better for kids to have two parents in the house, but there are other reasons to practice monogamy. If you think about it, the idea of monogamy really does go hand in hand with falling in love. You met your guy, you thought he was pretty cute, you went out on a few dates, then . . . Bam! You found yourself doodling hearts on your notebook like you did when you were fourteen. Or maybe you were texting little XOXOs or just spending every waking, nonworking hour with him.

So you've got one guy now, and you're his one and only girl. When he finds out he gets a promotion at work, he calls you first. He has those really, really great kisses that are saved only for you. And he has that kinky nickname he only uses when you're together between the sheets. Monogamy makes us feel special, and that is very, very sexy.

Monogamy in Hollywood
These relationships have made it in a land where your ultra-hot partner goes to work to kiss other people's ultra-hot partners on a regular basis.

10. *Will Smith and Jada Pinkett Smith (eleven years of marriage)*
 9. *Tim Robbins and Susan Sarandon (twenty-year relationship)*
 8. *Tom Hanks and Rita Wilson (twenty-one years of marriage)*
 7. *Goldie Hawn and Kurt Russell (twenty-six-year relationship)*
 6. *Danny DeVito and Rhea Perlman (twenty-seven years of marriage)*
 5. *Meryl Streep and Don Gummer (thirty-one years of marriage)*
 4. *Bill and Camille Cosby (forty-five years of marriage)*
 3. *Paul Newman and Joanne Woodward (fifty years of marriage)*
 2. *Alan and Arlene Alda (fifty-one years of marriage)*
 1. *Charleton Heston and Lydia Clark (sixty-three years of marriage)*

We Asked. **He Answered.**

We asked three guys from three cities and three walks of life what they thought about sex: Henry, who is in a five-year relationship and works as an actor in Los Angeles, California; David, a married father of two who works as a graphic designer in Cleveland, Ohio; and Kyle, who is in a one-year relationship and works as a writer/director in New York, New York. Throughout the book we'll let you in on their unique perspectives.

Q: What is better about being in a long-term relationship than being single?

A: *Being single kinda sucks if you are mental like I am. It's like eating crab. You have to put in way too much work for just a little bit of meat.* —DAVID

Assuming Monogamy and Happiness Are *Not* Mutually Exclusive

Go ahead and say it, your single friends are having way more fun than you are. You look around at the bar that you rarely go to anymore because you don't really drink to get drunk so much these days and realize that the jukebox hasn't been updated since the early nineties (before, you were too blitzed to notice Ace of Bass on repeat), and you think "those little blondes laughing giddily at the group of annoying frat boys are having a way better time than me!"

The fact of the matter is, sometimes it is good to be single, like in a crappy bar where there ain't much else to do but down 'em and flirt like hell. There are additional places where it is more fun to be single such as speed-dating events, mall food courts, and scuba lessons in the tropics where your instructor is mostly naked and smokin' hot. So, there it is, girls. There are times when the single life ain't so bad. But the fact is, sometimes it ain't so good. Let us refresh your memory:

- It is 4 P.M. on Thanksgiving Day as you heave your seventh scoop of stuffing onto your plate then sadly skulk back to the kids' table where your zitty seventeen-year-old cousin asks you if you want to share a joint after dinner. You say yes. You are single and sad.
- It is 9:30 on a Friday night when you spontaneously call everyone in your phone to make plans because it is warm and lovely and perfect for an outdoor cocktail. No one answers because they are all out on dates. You are single and sad.
- It's 8:30 on a Sunday morning, and you roll over and bump into nothing. Nothing at all. You are single and sad.

Why are we reminding you of these things? The fact is that sometimes, when we are feeling trapped on the wrong path, all it takes to make us feel less trapped is a trip down memory lane to remember other, less attractive paths we have been trapped on. This is not to say that you should stay in a relationship that is abusive to you or your partner in any way. Nor should you stay where you are hopeless and bored. But the very fact that you have picked up this book indicates to us that you are not totally done with your man. So, perhaps a quick reminder as to why some people call "Valentine's Day" "Violent-tine's Day" (trust us, someone calls it that . . .) might also solidify your desire to get your groove back in your relationship instead of abandoning ship.

Marriages that end in divorce in the United States only last an average of seven years according to several sources. For many, it seems real life gets in the way of the fairy tale. So if you are struggling with something like a seven-year itch—or two-year itch or twenty-year itch—you are not alone. But as a culture so used to being comfortable, what do we do with our discomfort? Well, we're glad you asked. We think you change it back to comfort.

To begin with, remember that even though we just told you that a lot of people bail on relationships, a lot of people don't. Look at your own family. Is anyone there in it for the long haul? How about your grandparents or even close family friends? Ask those people how they met and why they stayed together. Rachel, a guidance counselor from New York City, told us, "My parents have been married for forty years. My dad was supposed to be fixed up with my mom's friend and they all went swimming together. He fell in love with my mom because she got her hair wet in the ocean and the friend wouldn't."

Look around for stories like that one and this one from Randi, an editor in New York City: "My grandparents met during the war while they were hiding together in the forest. They conceived my mother during the war!" Use these romances as inspiration for wanting to make one out of your life with your guy—even if you met in a cubicle. We believe there *can* be romance under fluorescent lights, even if you had to take it into the supply closet to find it.

"I interviewed my grandparents before their fiftieth wedding anniversary," says Vanessa, a writer in Brooklyn, New York. "For my last question I asked how they made it fifty years. My grandfather replied wisely, 'Give a little. Always give a little,' and my grandmother said simply, 'Your grandfather turns me on.'"

Which brings us to the reason you are reading this book . . .

Sex is an important part of strengthening our relationships, but also to our well-being as individuals. Charles Kilpatrick, MD, an assistant professor of obstetrics and gynecology at the LBJ Hospital of the University of Texas in Houston, explains, "Masters and Johnson pioneered research efforts that expanded our scientific knowledge of the sexual response. They identified four stages of the sexual response: *excitement, plateau, orgasm and resolution.*" The Excitement Phase "is characterized by erotic feelings," says Dr. Kilpatrick. "The Plateau Phase heralds even more sexual tension and erotic feelings." The Orgasmic Phase brings on "a sudden release of the tension that has built up during the arousal and plateau stages," and "the Resolution Phase follows the orgasm with feelings of relaxation and well-being." And that sounds mighty fine to us.

 "I know nothing about sex because I was always married."

—Zsa Zsa Gabor

Eva Altobelli, MD, an addiction psychiatrist in New York City, explains further: "Endorphins are released during sex which are natural opiates in the brain. They are pain killers, and produce a sense of well-being. They are released during sex, physical contact, exercise, and other activities."

Remember endorphins? Those little guys are the same reason people feel great after going to the gym. They are proven to lower stress by lowering your blood pressure. A lot of research suggests that sex itself increases levels of important antibodies that protect you from getting sick and it can help you stay in shape. That is how it can benefit you as an individual. But as a couple, look at it this way, you probably share a home with your partner, or at least regularly share a bed as well as a social life and a remote control. By sharing a physical space for a few minutes a day, your relationship takes on something that no other relationship in your life can compete with: intimacy, both physical and emotional. A relationship without intimacy is like rich dark chocolate without the creamy peanut butter center, or as Kate, an accountant in Louisville, Kentucky, says, "It's like the chocolate without the chocolate!"

"It feels good to be touched," says Courtney, a yoga instructor in Portland, Maine.

Sasha, a guidance counselor in Jersey City, New Jersey, adds, "Not having sex creates a distance between you. Then you're just roommates."

Plus, isn't it obvious that as badly as you want to be wanted, he probably wants the same thing? So when you find yourself wondering if he thinks you smell funny or thinking he has started to look a little bit like a frog, someone is probably feeling unwanted. The prospect of rediscovering desire—his, yours, or both of yours—isn't an impossibility, but it also isn't as simple as opening up the jar of lube. In other words, if your relationship, over time, has evolved into something requiring the self-help section of the bookstore, it might be rife with complicated emotions, physical glitches, and changes. But there are ways to unearth them and then reinvent them all together.

In this book, we hope to arm you with tools to create a relationship that not only contains a lot of sex, but also contains a lot of desire. "Each individual needs to define for themselves what a healthy sex life is," says Lauree Ostrofsky, a life coach in New York

City. "Sex is a vital element to what makes a long-term commitment possible."

We will introduce you to women just like you from around the country—and even the world—who are in long-term relationships or have been in them and have come out full of advice for how they do it or how they would have navigated them differently. We will introduce you to experts, from therapists and life coaches to sex toy aficionados and physicians, all of whom will help you understand sex, sexual health, relationships, your body, and of course dildos and vibrating underpants. We will provide tips that will ensure a relationship that is sexy as hell.

Finally, this book will serve as a practical guide for a life together that is steamy and (mostly) drama-free—unless it's a drama about a nurse who comes to the aid of a foreign dignitary who has just foiled a plot for world domination and who is bruised and in need of a full, clothing-free medical work-up . . . or something.

Sex in relationships is a pretty complex subject, one we've chosen to approach honestly and, at times, bluntly, because, really, we know you don't want to be bullshitted. You just want to know how to make it happen in your own life. So here's what we've got for you.

CHAPTER 1

THE *SEXIFICATION* AND *DESEXIFICATION* OF RELATIONSHIPS

> When things began to fizzle with my first boyfriend during my freshman year of college, I found myself really starting to hate having sex with him, but I didn't know how to tell him. So I started mentally plotting which days I would have to do certain sexual favors out of obligation and which days I could have off. The system got pretty intricate. It probably would have been easier to just have a talk.

—Nina

Losing Our Collective Virginity

Remember in college, when the thing to do was to write down everyone you'd ever hooked up with so you'd have a master list of your conquests? We didn't do that either, we swear. We're just saying some *other* girls on our dorm floor did. Okay, so either this guy you're with is your first lover, or just the last one on the proverbial list. What exactly does your sexual history mean to your current relationship?

In a 2007 survey of American sexual behavior, women reported an average of four sex partners in a lifetime. But that number could be a little off, seeing how a similar survey from Durex reported that women in the United States average about *nine* sex partners. Who to believe? We're not real sure. For example, in New York City, the Durex number more than doubles: The *New York Daily News* recently reported that women in the Big Apple average twenty sexual partners. Whichever number you believe or hope is true, the fact is, most of us are having sex before we are married, which also means we are more likely to have sex with more than one partner in our lifetime.

Many of the women we spoke to admit that they kind of suspected that their first partner wasn't going to be their last. However, there were still a lot who'd held out for, if not great love, then at least a level of respect. Holly, an executive assistant in Repentigny, Quebec, had anticipated that having sex for her first time with just anyone would be a mistake. "I waited so damned long because I wanted to enjoy it with the right guy and not some slimy jock who was going to brag about it at school the next day," she said. "I was terrified of not being respected."

In her early relationships, Amina, an architect in Los Angeles, admits to limiting actual intercourse in favor of lighter bedroom play. "I opted for make-out sessions instead," she said. "Leaving them in pain was more fun."

Nina said, "I really wanted to be in love my first time, but I was nineteen and ready so I settled for feeling comfortable saying 'I love you,' even if I wasn't a hundred percent sure I meant it."

Whether your first sex partner wasn't your first, second, or any love, it certainly does look like a lot more women are ending up having had more than one bite of the poisonous apple that is love, doesn't it? So what does having had multiple partners and (ultimately) multiple relationship failures mean to us later in life, say, when we finally think we have found *the one?*

"More loves and partners means women have a better sense of what they want out of a relationship," says life coach Ostrofsky. So you're experienced. In this day and age, it doesn't mean you're cheap or slutty. It simply means you have a point of reference to compare your future relationships with.

Lina, a nurse in Edinburgh, Scotland, says, "I look at my boyfriend with a greater sense of appreciation having withstood my share of heartbreak."

Making sure you only allow healthy love affairs into your life is one way to make sure that none of your relationships are heavily destructive or get in the way of the great one that you end up committing to for life down the road. A great way to ensure that is to start off on the right foot.

Gloria, a Pilates instructor in New York, thinks that maturity is key. When it came to her first sexual relationship she says, "I knew I was not ready to have sex before I was seventeen. I'm happy to say that I knew that and didn't push it."

The truth is that everyone can emerge from sexual relationships unscathed no matter what age you start or how badly it ends as long as you know and respect your own limits. Nina says, "I knew what I would and would not do, and I was not afraid to do or not do it."

But with all these partners, how is it we are not all doomed to a life of cynicism and misery? Vanessa says something that sounds a lot like something we could get behind: "I think hope is the link that keeps me romantic," she said. "I always have hope in true love and that's why I can get over the ones that don't work out. I just stay pretty sure that the next one to come along will be it. And so far, he always has been."

"Anyway, to make a long, dull story even duller, I come from a time when a guy like me used to come into a joint like this and pick up a young chick like you and . . . call her a 'bimbo.'"

—Marlon Brando in *The Last Tango in Paris*

One-Night Stands

This book really is about long-term relationships, and recharging them, but it is our belief that we won't be able to make much headway into what can sometimes make our long-term relationships lose their spark without paying at least some attention to the spark itself. So let's start with the mythology, both good and bad of the one-night stand.

"I hate one-night stands because of the next morning awkwardness when I feel like trash," says Holly.

Nina says it simply and perhaps best: "When they're good they rock and when they're bad they suck."

We couldn't agree more. But why is that? First of all, let's look at what can make them great.

Judith Steinhart, a health and sexuality consultant in New York City, explains some of the history and the appeal behind the one-night stand:

> *In World War II they called it 'shore leave.' A woman would meet a sailor who was just there for one night. And you each could be yourselves because he didn't know you and you didn't know him. So what you'd have is this incredible intensity of feeling. You're not judging yourself. You're not worried about the next morning, because he's going to leave and for the first time perhaps you can be present with a man who is present with you.*

Like any first sex, a one-night stand means you also get to learn some new tricks for your proverbial bag of them. Then there is that feeling of safety clouded by the anonymity of it all. Certainly this holds true for things like vacation sex and sex on a business trip where both parties go into it knowing that it is a one-time shot.

Obviously, the lack of inhibition one feels in the heat of this kind of sex can also lead to the part of the one-night stand that sucks. You might wake up with the "What the hell was that?" feeling that can be so embarrassing the morning after.

You also may regret doing it because society tells you that sex with an almost stranger is wrong. "If someone had regrets, I'd ask them, What is it that they're regretting?" says Steinhart. "Are they regretting opening themselves? Are they regretting feeling disappointed? In what? Were they not present? Did they want to be with someone else? Did they prefer to see the other person the day after or the month after or for the rest of their lives?"

Anticipating mixed feelings, some women just choose not to have one-night stands. For Amina it has to do with self-respect. "I feel in complete control in the process of picking out the guy and manipulating him, but most men are so easy to bed that it has started to make me think that there really was no challenge and I just sucker myself."

Gloria says, "I like the thought of one-night stands. I wish I'd had the guts to have one before I was married. But I think I'm too caught up in body image to really let myself go—and confidently go after what I want—without knowing the person first."

A one-night stand can also be great for all the promise it holds. After all, maybe it will lead to a second night? And that passion, the awakening of something new, can be an excellent aphrodisiac.

Best One-Night Stands in Movies

Looking for some hot one-hit wonders? Check out these films' love scenes.

- **Most Romantic:** Ethan Hawke and Julie Delpy in *Before Sunrise*
- **Most Satisfying:** Anthony Michael Hall and the Prom Queen in *Sixteen Candles*
- **Most Redemptive:** Nicole Kidman and Jude Law in *Cold Mountain*

- **Most Optimistic for the Future:** Sarah Connor and the hot dude from the future in *The Terminator*
- **Most Likely to Get Your Bunny Boiled:** Michael Douglas and Glen Close in *Fatal Attraction*

Why Dating Is Fun

Of course, where one-night stands leave off is where dating comes in. Dating is the post-one-night-stand-pre-boyfriend/girlfriend time in the relationship when your phone rings and you get the kind of happy that looks dumb on the subway. You know, that shit-eating, idiot grin that makes strangers raise an eyebrow and look behind themselves to see what the hell is so amusing. It's that time when you make a little extra dinner in case he happens to swing by hungry so you can offer him something to eat . . . off of your naked body. And that's kind of the thing about the early days of dating: They're hot.

"There's just so much fill-in-the-blank-time there," says Nina.

We seem to fill in those blanks with sexy thoughts. After all, we don't know too many people who would infuse descriptions of the new guy they're seeing with characteristics like "farts while sleeping," and "sings Abba in the shower, badly." Instead we are more likely to prop them up with accolades like "that magical thing he does with his tongue must be something he always does really well in between reciting difficult Spanish poetry to roll his *r*'s and stay in shape. . . ." Yeah. Things like that.

Desire comes easily during this time in a relationship. Everything is new and exciting. Since you have a crush on the guy, even if he knocks your head into the headboard repeatedly during sex, you are likely to chalk it up to exuberant passion over sadistic tendency (depending on your opinion of sadism . . .). Either way, you are going to find it hot, or at least, full of potential. That is one basic difference between a long-term love and a crush. A crush manages to paint over all the bad things with a golden glow so that it seems like the best possible version of itself. A long-term love, on the other hand, acknowledges the flaws but maintains that underlying love. Both have their pros and cons. However, the fundamental problem with the crush is that after a while the flaws become harder to ignore. At its end you will either find a substantive love, or you will leave to go find another crush. Some people never want to give up the butterflies and the continued unknowing. Like Toby, an investigator in Columbus, Ohio, who says, "I was a serial dater prior to getting married, so I never had a relationship prior to marriage where it stayed good or bad over a period of time. I always hit the door first."

Toby is not that unusual. Dr. Altobelli explains, "What is happening in the brain when we are falling in love is the same in many ways as drug addiction. Neurotransmitters prevent the brain from reabsorbing some of those feel-good chemicals, thereby creating a sense of giddiness and general obsessiveness."

With all that rampant excitement flying around, it's hard to accept that it could end. The truth is, it may not end, but it will change. Unfortunately, as the newness begins to fade, a lot of women who don't hit the door begin to fake—maybe just faking feelings, but in fact, there are very few of us who haven't faked "it." Perhaps it has to do with women wanting to be pleasers. We want our men to feel like we want them as badly as they want us. So if our guy can reach orgasm in ten seconds, we want to follow suit. The broad problem here is that sometimes we can't time our orgasms perfectly. This isn't a waltz. No one's been choreographed. And then we feel bad. And then we fake orgasms. Holly said she has faked "to turn the guy on and keep him from feeling disappointed."

Gloria faked orgasms most often in the early part of her relationships. She said, "I think it was a combination of my lack of self-confidence, my lack of understanding how to ask for what I wanted sexually, and their lack of understanding of how to satisfy a woman sexually."

Other women we asked fake them when they are not enjoying the sexual experience. Toby said, "I have faked them just to get a guy the hell off of me."

We Asked. **He Answered.**

Q: *Have you ever been in a relationship where the sex wasn't very good? Did you try to improve it? How?*

A: I have tried to make suggestions regarding sex. I think the way I broach this subject most often is through "heat-of-the-moment" suggestion. Like when we're doing the "hokey-pokey" and I say, "turn yourself around." —KYLE

But some women categorically refuse to fake it, which we think is probably the best way to go, especially once you and your partner grow in your relationship to the point where each of you values the other's happiness. If you find you have trouble reaching orgasm because he doesn't know how to get you there, find a way to talk to him about it. We will go into ways to do so in Chapter 4. And if you can't convince your guy that you want him even if you can't come, let that be his own insecurity. We think it could be unhealthy to take that on yourself.

Amina said this, "I was honest when I couldn't have an orgasm on my meds. I just said, 'I can't come.'"

The Days Before You Could Pick the Smell of His Farts Out of a Lineup

There are things that just lose their appeal over time. Your brand-new lace bra loses a crocheted flower, your hot white-leather boots get scuffed and dingy, the cute new puppy pees on your sofa one too many times, and the list goes on. The same can be true of new relationships.

Sometimes, as with the peeing puppy, there are actual behaviors that lead to the loss of passion. Say your guy always gets into bed in his Star Wars flannel PJs or the number of comments he has made about your eating habits, like pointing out where those pancakes are going to land on your otherwise lovely frame, have just taken their toll. In cases like these, maybe the solution is simple: Hide the jammies and tell him to lay off the peanut-gallery observations.

In the case of the shine just coming off the love affair, the causes might prove more difficult to pinpoint. Of course, as we'll discuss in Chapter 2, sometimes the problems are chemical. Maybe if you just started a new birth control pill or are trying a different form of birth control altogether, the problem might simply require a little time for your body to adjust. If you feel you've given it enough time, maybe you need to try something new or go back to something tested.

Lifestyle shifts are often important to acknowledge as potential romance spoilers. "When we first got our dog," reports Vanessa, "that cold nose pressed to warm skin startled us out of a whole lot of smoochin'."

Sometimes big changes in your lives can also bring out big changes in the bedroom. From having kids to getting promoted, new stressors certainly affect our minds as well as our libidos. It is also possible that these stressors might go away or fade into the background but the changes might stick.

Such was the case for Vanessa and her guy. "The dog eventually stopped watching us have sex, but somehow the sex never went back to normal." (More on this in Chapter 5.)

If you think the problem might be physical, don't hesitate to see a doctor about it. You might be creating bigger problems for yourself by waiting. And don't be embarrassed. These people are trained to make you feel comfortable no matter how many times you show up with the Clap.

Still, frustration is absolutely warranted. The "Why us?" feeling that accompanies any slowdown in your sex life is rightfully aggravating. After all, your best friend just gave you an earful about the Saturday night she and her husband just pulled off in the laundry room—and the living room and the bathroom—of the boss's house at the company Christmas party. Your sister is calling to report on her hot new Italian lover. And your guy, although cute as anything despite his dulled stare at the football game and stinky feet up on the coffee table, is, well, pretty much about to get into bed next to you, assume the spoon position, and go to sleep. "But wouldn't it be nice?" you think. "Why them and not us?" you ask yourself.

One thing to remember, and this is important, is that just because his feet are, the fat lady ain't singing yet. Your passion *is* re-ignitable, and we think, somewhere deep inside, you believe it too.

Known Beasts vs. Unknown Monsters

Why do we stay? Why not simply throw him back and find a different fish? After all, these are the days of *lazy is the new effort* and what-not. "There comes a point in your life when other things besides sex are important, such as picking someone that would be a good partner forever," said Toby. She also mentions looking for a compatible roommate, someone who would make a good dad, and someone with similar life goals. None of those things require chiseled ass-cheeks and a well-placed smack upon them.

In terms of her guy's flaws, Courtney says, "I'd rather stay with the beast I know than go find a monster I don't."

That is one way of looking at it. If we know that the worst we are going to get is a random nose-pick in public, maybe that feels safer than getting a new guy and discovering that he likes to call waitresses, "Sugar."

We each choose our own nose-picker knowing that while everyone has some habit or vice that we may not love, our guy has an overall package that will keep us around.

Amina and her boyfriend of seven years have managed to have consistently great sex. We know. We hate her too. (She also has amazing hair. Bitch.) She said simply, "You know when you find your puzzle piece ;)." (Yeah, she typed that little winky face too.) But there is more to her story. Keeping things hot does not usually happen without some kind of effort. "Having sex the same way gets boring," she says. "You've got to have variety in the time of day or night, the kind of foreplay, that sort of thing. I flat-out tell him what has turned me on, and he takes the bait! But what turns me on varies, so there's your variety."

Anticipating that both of you have a responsibility to your sex life is as important as remembering to take the recyclables to the curb on Tuesday nights or to get the report in to your boss on time. Buying this book was a great first step. Reading it, an even greater step! Now, before you take out a vibrator with rotating beads and scare the hell out of everybody, let's begin with learning why you are *already* compatible with your guy.

CHAPTER 2

FINDING *COMPATIBILITY* WITH HIM— *IN AND OUT* OF BED

> I once went out with a guy who was perfect on paper. He had a job, owned a house, took me on real adult dates—plays, dinner, wine tastings. He was wonderful in every way, but I just wasn't feelin' it. I found myself avoiding a goodnight kiss and only making plans with him when there was nothing else going on—terrible!
>
> —Missy

The Good-on-Paper Guy

He's driven, fascinating, the right age, living in the same area code, and not embarrassing to introduce to your friends. So, what gives? You should be trying to tear his clothes off, not patenting excuses that make the classic headache look like an invitation to get naked. But the truth is, the idea of sex with him gives you a headache.

"A relationship without sex is called friendship," warns Ostrofsky. "Sex is a vital element to what makes a long-term commitment possible."

She ain't kidding. And we're pretty sure you also agree or you wouldn't be joining us for this stroll down sexual-chemistry lane. So what can you do when your guy has everything but the I-want-you gene?

Science knows so much about the secretion of a sex hormone in female animals called pheromones that they are even able to bottle it for use in pest control. However, it wasn't until the mid-1980s that anything was known about pheromones in people. In an article published in the *Washington Post* in 1986, the headline read, "Pheromones Discovered in Humans." Less than one month later, *Time Magazine* published an article which read, "Studies find that male pheromones are good for women's health."

Dr. Altobelli, whose field of study generally focuses on the effects of chemicals in the body, explains, "There have been studies that prove the pheromone receptors in humans are generally specific." In other words, we are built to be attracted to other humans and not, like, dogs or cats, 'cause that'd be weird. She further explains, "It also means 'I am attracted to pheromones that are *similar* to my father's, but not my father's.'"

So, now you're thinking, "Our pheromones must not match up. Well, nothing we can do about a scientific truth." But wait one second before you cry "hormone" and throw in the towel. Let's think for a moment about what pheromones are and how they work.

Dr. Kilpatrick says that pheromones are "a type of ectohormone secreted by an individual and perceived by a second individual of the same species, thereby producing a change in the sexual or social behavior of that individual."

Hormone release is cyclical, but it is also mental. In other words, when you are aroused, you secrete more hormone than when you are not aroused. We all know that sometimes going from "not-aroused" to "aroused" requires only minutes and a few mental images of Brad Pitt's six-pack in *Thelma and Louise*. You simply have to *decide* to picture those mental images. Therefore, it is possible to say that you have some control over what smells you are secreting—and maybe even a modicum of control over that which is being secreted by your man.

Dr. Altobelli agrees, "Pheromones in women are released through sweat, with the highest concentrations in the armpit." There are also times of the month when they are stronger, she says. "In women, pheromones change with the menstrual cycle. When women are more fertile, they are generally more potent."

There is also evidence that some people become more chemically attracted to their partner over time. Marie says, "My current relationship started out with a 'not so good' sex life. But as time went on and we became more familiar with each other, it has gotten sooo great!"

Explanations for this phenomenon run the gamut. Obviously, over time people become less inhibited with one another. Some women find they are less shy about expressing their needs. Others are simply less embarrassed about making the inevitable orgasm faces in front of their man. But there are more subtle changes that happen over time.

Confidence and intimacy can help create desire. Dates early on in the relationship can sometimes prove poor indicators of a person's actual self. Things like nerves, excitement, and bad hairstyles might make it hard for you to see that underneath that pink button down (him, not you) there is a great and very sexy man. Maybe it will take until the moment he grabs you around the waist to move you out of the way of oncoming traffic that you will see, and feel, exactly what this man has to offer.

Marie went on to say, "It's amazing now. Sometimes I just look at my husband and get butterflies."

And if that doesn't work, get working on those orgasms. As Dr. Altobelli tells us, "Oxytocin is a hormone secreted from the pineal gland in the brain, by the hypothalamus during orgasm. It makes one feel 'in love.'"

We're not sure we buy this theory 100 percent. Orgasm can't always mean love. We mean, we're not falling in love with our showerheads any time soon. But, who can argue with a few extra Os? (That's what Chapter 4 is for.)

"What Turns You On?"

We asked women what they found most attractive about their men. Here's what they said:

"He doesn't have to be a Wall Street banker, but that'll work." —ROXIE, TEACHER, NEW YORK CITY

"I had never thought that power would be something I'd be attracted to, but holy shit! It's intoxicating." —RANDI

"People that can keep track of their finances. I find those people very attractive." —COURTNEY

"When he cooks for you!" —VALERIE, EDITOR AND WRITER, QUEENS, NEW YORK

"I love it when my guy kisses my neck and back. Makes me go crazy!" —TARA, PHOTOGRAPHER, BALTIMORE

Cultivating Chemistry

So let's look at your relationship now. You are thinking, "But we've been together *forever* and he has that comb-over!" But here's the thing, are you guys fostering confidence in each other? Has your relationship become a nitpicking fest? Does he defer to you for every decision? Or vice versa? Perhaps what is missing isn't chemical after all. Maybe it is psychological. Remind yourself, if chemistry and psychology are related, maybe it's time to focus on the positives.

Create an environment that cultivates confidence. Remember, it isn't only for him, but for you too. "I found myself being critical of everything about him," says Gretta, a theater producer in Prague.

"In retrospect, it's funny that I ever wondered why he stopped wanting to have sex with me!"

This phenomenon can certainly work both ways. Perhaps he will begin to feel less confident and therefore less attractive and attract*ed*, or perhaps you will begin to allow these flaws you point out to detract from your wanting him. Try offering your man one good compliment a day. Don't make it up—really look for the best things about him and tell him about it. Or if you are feeling picked on, let him know. Sometimes it's as easy as lightening the mood like Vanessa does: "When he harshes on me I let him know that he can have that one jab, but he has to follow it up with two compliments."

Two compliments for every one criticism sounds fair. But if his mood swings and running commentary are something that you feel has begun to take its toll on you, you might want to consider that you are in an unhealthy relationship. Let him know, not that he is a bad person, but that you are unhappy in the dynamic you two have created. Sometimes it's easier to elicit change from a person when we can admit to our own culpability in the situation. You have allowed him to criticize you, but now you are going to help to stop it. If he seems amenable to change, your relationship is salvageable. If he fights it, perhaps you should consider getting out.

Another thing to watch out for is whether or not one person dominates every decision the two of you make. Roxie says this about being attracted to a man, "A lot of times people start losing their luster after you start seeing that they are not as powerful as they first seemed." Maybe once you snagged your steady, he turned into a "whatever you say" kind of guy. Those guys might grow less exciting because, frankly, it's akin to dating the doormat. And while he might metaphorically read "Welcome" across his woven yellow face, you are wiping your feet all over it.

If this is the case, try going on a strike from decision-making. You might find that you have a few control issues of your own and that having an opinion about *everything* is what's encouraging the rollover attitude. Let him choose the restaurant and the movie for a change. Ask him to plan a date night. Don't offer your input unless it is to point out what you are enjoying as you go.

If, on the other hand, you are the wet noodle around the house, gird up your inner core and make a plan! Choose the place and time of your next date night, ask him to bottle the negatives and search for the positives in your decisions and watch your confidence (and maybe your pheromones) soar.

Great Expectations

Another way to begin transforming your sex life is by changing your expectations. Let us repeat that: *Change* your expectations. We do not mean lower them or leave them out all together. We just mean that maybe you are thinking of your relationship in the wrong way. Perhaps you imagine your guy in a way that you have been conditioned to think of him—like he should be the knight in shining armor who not only says all the right things but opens the car door for you and sends enough roses to fill up your entire apartment for no reason at all. Okay, so maybe he did not sashay out of the movie screen at your neighborhood

Cineplex. But that doesn't mean he isn't every bit the hot number you want him to be.

"Try to imagine him with someone else," suggests Nina. "Think about it, if you broke up and ran into him with someone else—it's an instant aphrodisiac."

Also along these lines, let us suggest that you make a point of noticing the reactions of other women when you are out with your guy. "Seeing another woman check out your man can be the hottest thing in the world," says Allison, an English professor in Eugene, Oregon.

"You can't expect your partner to provide for every need," says Ostrofsky. Therefore, make sure you evaluate what is truly important in a partner. Then, consider whether or not you have realistic expectations for your guy. Is he respectful of you? Does he know what *he* wants but is willing to consider *your* wants in his decisions? Maybe he is a slob, but does he seem to hear you when you express frustration at having to put away his stinky gym shoes for the tenth day in a row? If you basically answered yes to those questions, perhaps there are other areas where your man doesn't measure up. Maybe you cannot stand one more conversation about cars, or you are frustrated that he won't gossip about his friends' love lives with you. Of course, having a friendship with your man is important, but understand that it is healthy to have more than one relationship, each of which can fulfill different needs. "My grandmother once said, 'Don't make your man your girlfriend. You have girlfriends for that,'" says Nina.

Perhaps by having new expectations of your guy, your disappointments will be lessened and your libido will rise.

"It's not the men in my life that counts—it's the life in my men."

—Mae West

Out of the Box

Maybe right now you two are in a cozy little igloo. There's nothing wrong with the igloo. It's comfortable, safe, and warm. But, dude, it's freaking boring in that igloo. You're cooped up. So why not go out together and play in the snow? Sure, you might get a little chilly, but believe us, it will be a rockin' good time.

Lame metaphors aside, you're going to have to step out of your comfort zone if you want to boost the chemistry factor between you and your guy.

"To keep your relationship exciting you should try new things and be spontaneous," suggests Marie.

"Try not to get in a rut," agrees Sasha. "Do new things that aren't part of your typical routine, like dates, trips and getaways, concerts, marathons—whatever you can think of."

"My boyfriend and I love to travel," says Valerie. "One time we casually talked about taking a weekend trip to Philadelphia. And the next day, he called to say he wanted to go that weekend. We ended up buying the train tickets and booking a hotel right then and there!"

Sounds pretty romantic, huh? By changing the status quo a bit and doing something unexpected and exciting, Valerie and her boyfriend have successfully lit a flame underneath their relationship.

"Romance is easy—or should be—at the beginning of relationships, because everything is new," says Ostrofsky.

As much as we don't want to become one of those old, boring couples, we can start to resemble one fast. Because we're not putting as much into the romance of the relationship as we once did. And while romance might have come easy in the beginning, you might have to work a bit at it to get it back once you've been together for a while.

"When it's not easy anymore, you two have to get creative," says Ostrofsky. "This is where communication and trust really come in handy, because it'll take both of you working together to figure it out."

She adds: "Changing the status quo can mean being radical or challenging the norm. If your couch faces the TV, turn it around one night and see how it changes the conversation. If you think you know the answer to a question, ask it in a new way and really listen to the answer."

That may even mean spending time apart here and there, like Lucy, a pharmacist in Toronto, does: "I make time to do my own thing. Absence makes the heart grow fonder. Each reunion injects new love and passion and helps me re-appreciate what I have." Plan a girls' night, take a class—we're not saying to avoid your guy altogether, but take just a little time to focus on yourself, which may make focusing on your relationship a little easier when you're back together again.

Maybe you and your guy can't hop a flight this weekend. But that doesn't mean you can't inject some romance in little, subtle ways that feel exciting and new.

"I really like to be flirted with, and when we go out, he will tell me I look pretty or give me a kiss when he walks by," says Missy.

This works both ways, so go ahead and flirt with your guy! If *you* want to be flirted with, why not initiate it? It can be something as little as a kiss or as big as surprising him when he comes home from work by wearing some lingerie . . . or by wearing nothing at all.

Then, once you're in bed, remember to keep the chemistry alive. "Do things for your partner that you want done for you," says Sasha. "Be grateful and don't take their efforts for granted."

"My husband and I respect each other's wishes and are willing to try what the other wants, without making fun of each other," says Laura, a director in Pittsburgh. "Additionally, we talk to one another, and really listen. We show we are interested in the other's thoughts, values, and wants."

Sasha adds: "It's especially important to try new things in your sex life, like toys, positions, and places."

"We buy books on new positions, we buy toys to use, anything that is new and different," says Laura. "Once we were in a bookstore's relationships section. There were two teenagers sitting on the floor looking at the pictures in a book of different sexual positions. The young woman said to the guy, 'That looks painful.' I glanced down and saw it was a position we'd tried. I said, 'It was, but it may be because of our age.' The look the two of them gave us was priceless." So what if you're in the thick of it and the chemistry's just not happening? You may have to get out of your head a little bit.

"I use my imagination. Sometimes I picture us outdoors, or in a stairwell or somewhere where people might walk in," says Melissa W., a writer in Brooklyn, New York. "Though we're always just in our bedroom, the imagination helps."

"A woman needs to figure out how she can 'get there' herself," says sexpert Steinhart. "You have an opportunity to change your mindset. Get a whole variety of things and see what works."

So what we wanted to know is: Can chemistry be taught? Even without memorizing the periodic table of elements?

Well, it seems that yes, it can. Listen, you've deemed this relationship worthy enough to do a little reading about how to improve it. So we're thinking that you believe it's worth it to stick it out despite any chemistry issues.

One thing that you might have to deal with is your physical attraction—it's true that it can wane a bit. So how do you get it back?

The fact is, chemicals are mixed together to make compounds. If your man, covered in manure from six hours in the horse barn, doesn't do it for you, try to add or replace some of the changeable parts. Sure, you have to deal with his ridiculously long earlobes, but you can always tell him that his hair looks better when he grows it long—or give him some animal-magnetism-type cologne. That's sure to distract you from, if not the Dumbo ears, at least the Dumbo smells.

The moral here is that whatever's bugging you can be improved. If it's something that he could be sensitive about, don't go out and blurt it—be subtle. Maybe even encourage change on both of your parts.

"Join a gym, or do a charity walk together, so you both get in better shape and thus increase attraction," suggests Sasha. Whether or not your bodies change, just participating in those physical activities could take you both from zero to horny.

"It's just a basic tenet that if you are in good shape, your sex should be better," says Dr. Kilpatrick.

Another way the chemistry might be off could be related to your personalities. In addition to criticisms and judgments we mentioned earlier in the chapter, perhaps you two have been getting on each other's nerves in other ways lately. Is one of you crankier than normal? Do you feel like you just aren't seeing each other in the soft rosy glow of your early crush days? Maybe one of you is even feeling sort of "over it."

"I think communication is the key," says Marie. "If things are bothering you, you need to talk and not let things blow up."

Melissa W. believes that turning things around simply takes some positivity. "I recommend laughing," she says. "I think having foreplay that's affectionate and appreciative goes a long way, too. Tickling, being complimentary, and the like are all positive."

When personalities aren't clicking, the frequency with which you two have sex could suffer. And, well, when you're not getting some, you can get crankier—and so can he. And then the crankiness escalates and escalates and escalates. . . . It's sort of a catch-22.

"If it's been awhile—you know what I mean—we are just totally blunt with each other," says Missy. So, how does it work when one person says to the other, "Hey, I'm really horny because we haven't done it lately?" According to Missy, it totally works: "All of a sudden we'll go from zero to sixty and remember how fun it is to get it on!" she says.

If you are suffering from a case of the "just not feeling it" let us remind you, relationships are cyclical. Changing your mindset and the things about your man you notice can help tremendously. You obviously suspect that, or you probably wouldn't be reading this book. "I keep a list of things that Aaron does that make me feel good or impressed by him," says Vanessa. "Sometimes I just read it to remind myself what a catch I have." That's not a bad idea. The next time he wows you, write it down and read it from time to time as a reminder.

If, however your partner is the one pulling away, this can feel frustrating, or even like a devastating turn of events. We cannot force people to love us. But we can take a minute, release our choke-hold and give everyone a chance to breathe. If communication isn't working, remind yourself that the sexiest thing in the world is a self-contained, confident person who does not run around the room saying over and over, "Why don't you love me!?" while crying and pounding their fists on the table. No, that is not sexy. Not sexy at all. Our advice in this case is counterintuitive. Instead of jumping up and down to get noticed, leave. Sometimes absence really does make the heart grow fonder. We don't mean leave for good, just get really busy. When you see him, rather than discussing him or your floundering "us," tell him with gusto all the interesting things you've been doing. Then go read a book in a very sexy negligee. You have no idea how loud that kind of silence can be.

Get Outta Here: Best Affordable Weekend Getaways
- Find a rental in a wooded area outside the city you live in. Try to choose a place with good hiking, skiing, or swimming.
- Camping. Watching him build a fire is all the kindling you'll need for a hot night.
- Find good hotel rooms in your own city. Just make sure you choose one with a big bed, a hot tub, and room service.

- Toss your maps and take a road trip anywhere! Worry about where you'll stay when you get there. Or, if everything's sold out or too expensive, drive all night back home. Then stay in bed all day the next day.
- Set up your mattress in your living room. Break out a bunch of games and movies and spend the day in bed. Order in and don't worry about crumbs. You can change the sheets tomorrow. Hopefully they'll need it anyway!

Myths and Truths about Saving Yourself

Chemistry, as you know, is different with each partner. Wait. There's a chance that maybe you don't know. If you waited for love until you had sex, then maybe you've only had one or two or three sexual partners. So if you don't have much—or anything—to compare it to, and your chemistry with him is questionable, do you owe it to yourself to have sex with other people?

Not necessarily. It may be totally tempting. There are hot guys everywhere. Maybe one of them would be a crazy good roll in the hay.

We'd like to remind you of the operative word here, *love*. That's why you waited. And that's what you've got. Appreciate it. Remind yourself of all the reasons that waiting was important to you. Let these women remind you:

"One pro for saving yourself is staying disease-free," says Heather, a veterinarian from Phoenix. "This is becoming more and more important nowadays, especially with HPV and HSV, both diseases that stay with you for life."

"I saved myself for love and, really, so did my husband," says Missy. "We have not slept with many people at all, and I think it matters. It feels good knowing that he hasn't slept with any of our friends or people that we may run into. It especially felt good in the beginning of the relationship because then I knew he wasn't just in it for the sex."

Heather thinks that more experience doesn't always equate to better sex. "I don't think I really learned anything from previous sex partners that I could not have discovered with my husband," she says.

In fact, love can bring a certain passion and intimacy to the bedroom—something that might not exist with someone you have lukewarm feelings about. No matter how much like Lenny Kravitz they look.

"Sex is a great way to connect with someone you care about, and being in love makes you feel good about doing it," says Missy.

"I don't think I could just do it without having any emotional attachment," says Marie.

"Sex with someone you love is much more special and fulfilling. Of course that doesn't mean it has to be boring!" says Valerie.

In fact, saving yourself really doesn't have to influence your future sex life at all. It certainly hasn't for Amy, an editor in Lyndhurst, New Jersey, who says, "Even though I have only had one partner, I am still a very sexual person."

This is what we think: In the case of your sex life, quality trumps quantity. If you are in a relationship where the sex is mediocre, it is easy to blame a lack of experience. However, the remedy, again, in our humble opinion, is that you can get that experience just as easily *with* the man you love than by running out to the nearest bar and flirting your way into the bed of the hot (and we'll assume well-experienced) bartender. What you already share with your man—a level of trust and comfort—you will not have with said-bartender. And while you might get to try the Seventh Posture of Burton's *The Perfumed Garden* with the bartender faster than if you took the time to come to it organically with your man, you also might have avoided the inevitable whiplash that comes to the impatient and the almost definitely out of their league.

We Asked. **He Answered.**

Q: We're not into the rolling over and falling asleep business after sex. How can a girl ask for more pillow talk/cuddle time?

A: Don't have sex right before bed. Have sex before you go out for the evening. Then you're awake and sprightly and much more likely to avoid this whole "rolling over and going to sleep" nonsense. *—HENRY*

For Those of You Who Have Done Dallas

Okay, so if you're reading this, and you're like, "What the hell? I didn't save myself. It wasn't like the whole football team or anything, but I think by now I could put one together if I gathered them onto one field. . . . Are you saying I put my, um foot in it?" No, we're not. You've got good stuff going for you too. Every woman is different, and what's right for each woman is different. Having a few notches on your bedpost probably means you've experienced a few things you have forgotten all about, either by choice, alcohol, or shame. Now, however, we beg you to try to mine those parts of your life where the sex felt great. Imagine using some of those special tricks the guy who refused to take off the green glittery sock hat taught you with the man you love right now who doesn't wear, well, sock hats to bed. See what happens if you implement a few of those maneuvers. Or what about the guy who could do that thing to your earlobe that made you purr? Whip that nugget out for good measure!

"Variety is the spice of life!" says Valerie. "It's good to be able to learn things from different lovers—or teach them a few things. *Safe* sex, of course!"

"I have had some great sex with some interesting people that otherwise would have been lost," says Heather.

Missy points out that even less-than-perfect sexual experiences can be beneficial down the line. "I still cringe at some of the things past partners have done and it makes me appreciate my husband more," she says.

That is an excellent point. On top of recreating the hot moments, you can apply the cringe-worthy moments to the list of things that make *him* your Prince Charming.

"This one dude's large sweat droplet fell into my open mouth. Plop. Sorry, but it went plop and it's therapeutic for me to tell you that . . ." says Nina.

Some people do think having more than one partner in a lifetime was an important part of their development into a sexually mature person. Rachel says, "I definitely think it allows you to figure out what you need both from a sexual perspective and a relationship perspective. It can help you convey what works for you sexually."

"I think it's individual, but it was *definitely* important for me to sample a few goods before settling down," says Melissa W. "I think I would've always wondered what other people and circumstances were like, and I would've driven myself crazy wondering if I hadn't tried things out."

Sasha says she was once in a relationship and found herself wondering what else was out there. When the relationship ended, she was happy to sow some wild oats. "Next time I'm in a committed relationship," she says, "I will have gotten it out of my system."

"I think that with each partner you learn something about yourself and who you are," says Marie. "You have so many emotions and connections during a sexual relationship that as silly as it sounds, you grow more. I know after each relationship that I had learned different things about me and about life."

So, yes, through sex, you've learned about yourself. And, the more you've learned about yourself, the better sex you'll be able to have. You'll know what turns you on, what positions you like, what kinds of moves can lead you to orgasm. And, well, it's probably been pretty fun. Now is the time to put those experiences to good use. By remembering the tricks of relationships past, you are accessing the wisdom you already have. One thing, though: Maybe don't tell your guy that the thing you do with your tongue that makes him howl was your ex-boyfriend's favorite too.

CHAPTER 3

STAYING **MONOGAMOUS** . . . AND TRUSTING **HIM** TO

> My husband lied to me about his porn use for two years while telling me constantly that he hated porn. He volunteered a hatred for porn, and I found out years later that he had an addiction to it. It almost ruined our marriage.

—Morgan

Pookie vs. Snookums

What is it about using words like "boyfriend," "fiancé," and "husband" that can sometimes change everything about a relationship? "Giving a name to your relationship makes you face a reality you may not have looked at yet," explains Ostrofsky. "To do so requires you both to decide if you're ready for something more and if you want it with *this* person."

On top of that, naming adds the collective connotation of a word to your relationship. So, if you went from saying "that dude that just went to the bathroom" to "my boyfriend," suddenly you must attach the meaning of that word to him as well. For Amanda, a project manager in Washington, D.C., getting to the B/G-words was easy. "We were sixteen years old when we started dating. Pretty much once we had been seen holding hands in public, the terms 'boyfriend' and 'girlfriend' were bestowed."

No matter their age, a lot of people just wait until the term is applied to them rather than going ahead and suiting up with the words "Jesse's Girl" across their chests. Laura, who had just come out of a divorce when she met her guy, never used the word at all. "My parents just knew he was my boyfriend when I moved in with him."

Applying those terms however can be important because it indicates that you are ready to claim one another and move forward together as a team. Once you know—if not by word of mouth then at least in your heart—that you are sharing a monogamous relationship, the feeling inherent to your relationship is likely to deepen. If that is not the case, and suddenly one or both of you finds yourself in something akin to a full-blown panic, you may not be ready to be involved with your guy at this level.

Once you are confident in your status as a couple, however, it isn't a bad idea to notice ways in which your intimacy with each other is unique. For example, Amanda explains, "I like to sit in his lap and recline like he's a chair while we're watching TV in bed. Hard to describe, but it feels really good. It's like being totally surrounded by him."

Amy cuddles with her man to achieve nonsexual intimacy. But they also play together. "We like to laugh a lot together. And now we have [the video game] Rock Band . . ." she says.

If your own relationship lacks nonsexual intimacy, perhaps this is the root of the problem with your *sexual* intimacy. We recommend you carve out time together to just be still together. If you go out to a movie with him, take his hand and remember to stroke it periodically. A small move like that can instantly reconnect and rejuvenate any romance, even an old, worn-out one. If you have kids, hectic jobs, unwieldy pets, or all three, maybe you only have time for quickies. As for pillow talk, you wonder, what kind of sweet nothings will he fall for after you tell him yet again this morning that he needs to deal with his own dirty underwear?

"I tell him all the time when we are laying together in bed that I love his eyes or arms," says Vanessa. "Sometimes, if I think he thinks I am getting too cheesy I throw in that he'd be really cute if he didn't look so much like Big Bird."

Using your words to remind your guy that he is attractive to you is a great way to boost the intimacy between you, even if you aren't a girl who falls for the one-liners and needs to keep it light. No matter how busy you are, sneaking in a compliment doesn't have to take hours, dignity, or even nudity.

"Just whisper it to him if you are standing in the middle of a crowded room," suggests Vanessa.

In fact, we think the same can happen in a crowded house, or even in the middle of the night when you return from the bathroom. Imagine if your guy pointed out every great thought he had about you. Would you get sick of it? We didn't think so . . .

Making a Man(tain) out of a Mole(hill)

So now that the issue of using your words is on the table, let us remind you that they can be used for good or evil. Obviously we can help create intimacy in our relationships by telling our guys how great they are and pointing out for them all their best qualities. Having a partner who knows you are on his side and wholly in love with him is comforting. Unfortunately intimacy can sometimes create complacency. Complacency stems from that feeling that there is little you can do or say (or not do or say) to rattle the incredibly sturdy foundation of your relationship. But the truth is that little jabs, such as constant reminders of past loves or how much better a dancer your best friend's boyfriend is, can and will chip away at that foundation. An even greater risk is when your complacency leads to hubris, and you start to act out in ways that betray your man's trust.

Leanne, a copywriter in New York City, told a story about a friend who said she'd made a mixed tape for another guy and wanted to know if that was cheating. Leanne replied fairly, "It depends what songs you put on it."

That's the thing. You are the only one who can judge the meaning behind your words and behaviors. Consider whether having a close but platonic relationship with someone of the opposite sex is cheating. Courtney said, "I think we'd all agree that you'd feel betrayed if your partner was paying all of this special attention to someone else."

Gauging your behaviors by how you would feel if the roles were reversed is a great way to figure out whether your choices cross the line. But perhaps you are like Simona, a theater producer in San Francisco, who says, "My boyfriend lets me get away with *everything* and sometimes it makes me want to continue to test him, to see how far I can go."

We Asked. **He Answered.**

Q: *Why do you think some men aren't big on compliments? How can a woman successfully milk her share of good compliments out of a guy?*

A: I think most people, not just guys, don't really get how important compliments are to people. We spend so much time worrying about ourselves that we forget to share the love—it's a "Me"-generation thing. Can a woman drag compliments out of a guy? Yes. But I think the only way to do it without causing trouble, is to have a mutual friend sit the guy down for a talk. That friend could say: "Don't you think _____ looks pretty? Well, tell her!"
—KYLE

If that is the case, perhaps your guy is struggling with insecurity issues. Maybe you need to consider that you are testing the wrong boundaries. Instead of seeing how far your guy will bend before he snaps, see instead how he will thrive if you push him to recognize his power and greatness as a man. Sometimes, the way we treat our partners is a self-fulfilling prophecy. So, instead of giving out your number to a handsome stranger in front of your guy and his best friend, give your guy a little under-the-table foot action and watch his confidence soar.

"Be your best self in your relationship," says Steinhart. "Your goal is to build the best relationship you can so no one feels desperate."

The Importance of Being Honest

When navigating new love affairs, most people just instinctively recognize certain rules. Even if the two of you have the kind of connection where you could talk all night about everything, you will probably avoid the battle you fought with pubic lice in 2004 and the night you spent puking in your ex-boyfriend's lap while giving a blow-job after drinking too much alcohol (unless you have a really hilarious way of telling it that starts with "My friend . . ."). But what happens six months, one year, two years later? Interesting tidbits about your past are slim pickins. And he just mentioned that he's never ever dated *anyone* who has *ever* had an STD as he casually winds his spaghetti around his fork and sucks it up. Your brain struggles between two thoughts, "Tell him you had pubic lice because it's the honest thing to do," and "Abort Mission! TMI!" What do you do?

Ostrofsky suggests that you look at it like this: "What use will revealing the information serve you? If it's just out of curiosity, let it go. At best, it's no big deal. At worst, one or both of you are left jealous, angry, or embarrassed."

If you're not prepared to unload your entire sexual history, and he asks you what "your number" is, Steinhart recommends saying, "Some experiences have been successful. Some have been less successful. Some have been painful. Some have been lovely. I've learned a lot over time."

However, if you feel like you need to reveal the number of people you have shagged in a concrete digit—or digits—to your guy, be prepared to allow him his reaction, whatever it might be.

"I told my guy my number of sex partners, and he totally freaked out. Then I was pissed that he was pissed because I felt judged," says Vanessa.

"Is your boyfriend supposed to absolve you of that?" asks Steinhart. "Really, what did you expect would happen?" The thing to consider is how much of the anger is about the other person; in other words, your man might feel more pressure to be "better" now that he knows how much competition he's had. This is not about you. And reacting as though you are being judged may also be because you judge yourself.

"In the end," Vanessa continues, "I realized that I feel really okay with my sexual past, and after I spent some time letting him know how much I love having him as my lover, we both totally got over it."

If he tells you something shocking from his past, the best thing to say is "thank you for telling me," says Steinhart. 'Nuff said.

So, while we do suggest avoiding certain difficult topics of conversation if they will only lead to fruitless frustration and sorrow, we also think there are times when it is important to talk to your guy about delicate issues. Say for example your ex is in town. He has phoned and wants to meet you for a drink to catch up. We understand that is something you might really want to do. If in your heart you believe your guy will really suffer unnecessarily if he knows—and the fact is, he probably wouldn't even want to know—we understand that you might decide not to tell him. But then, imagine the consequences if his coworker mentions the next day that she saw you at Ruby Tuesdays having an appletini with a great-looking guy. You see our point.

Instead of either (a) lying to your guy or (b) breaking your guy's heart, we want to encourage you to have a very real conversation about this with him before it even happens. In other words, bring up the question of whether he'd ever go get a drink with an ex. Then start laying the foundation for an establishment of rules. If by the end you both agree that you trust each other enough to keep any such meetings to a single drink and then a polite hug goodbye, it is okay not to mention it. Or perhaps you will decide that you'd like to know the plan, and you'd be grateful for a quick check in before and after, which may keep you from worrying unnecessarily. Now, if your guy makes a formal decree that you are to close your eyes if you even bump into that asshole on the street, the choice is yours. You can lie to your man, but be aware of what you are putting at stake. Then you might want to spend some time focusing on your man's trust issues by pointing out how trustworthy you are. If however, you do go for the lie, then let us suggest you meet someplace with a different area code, and wear sunglasses and a wig.

When Harry Met Sally

Setting up rules and boundaries is also a great technique for keeping the peace between you and your man when it comes to close friendships with members of the opposite sex, including exes. We can't deny that we've all had some of our most valuable relationships with people that at some point or other we have been sexually attracted to. This might pose a threat to your relationship, but there are also ways to create great and valuable relationships with your past romantic interests as a couple.

Susan, a program director in New York City, says, "My ex-boyfriend's girlfriend actually wanted me at his bachelor party because she said she knew I'd look after the whole thing."

We think that that girlfriend was on to something. By befriending your guy's gal pals, you will remove the scariest thing of all about trust issues: the unknown. By forging a relationship with your guy's female friends, you might discover that they are the best allies you have in your relationship, and new good friends for you!

Nina says, "After I got to know his best friend, Emily, I realized she was better than a guy friend for him because she let him talk about our relationship and get a handle on his feelings. Because she really likes me, she usually takes my side and helps to get my point across."

The same is true for Laura and her guy friends. "I need their male insight to help me understand my husband," she says. "It is wonderful, actually, since they can tell me clearly why a guy does the things he does. Since there is different emotional involvement with them, I can unemotionally understand what is going on."

On the other hand, sometimes helping your guy to accept your guy friends can be more of a challenge. If this is the case, Steinhart recommends asking yourself and your guy, "What is he so worried about? You are choosing to be with *him*."

If he just finds it really hard to reconcile your relationship with exes, you might want to be more selective with your information. Vanessa says, "My way of staying friends with the people I have slept with in the past is to never admit I have slept with them in the past."

If your guy already knows about your past, and despite spending time with you and your guy friends, still doesn't like your relationships with them, perhaps you need to think about the possibility that your behavior is disrespectful to your guy. Are you unintentionally flirtatious? Sometimes we choose our friends of the opposite sex because we subconsciously enjoy attention from them that becomes inappropriate once we couple up. Other times, we might not see it that our "harmless" guy friends really, really want to get in our pants. In those cases, it might be up to you to make it clear to your friend that your friendship has changed now that you are in a serious relationship and that he can call when he is happily in a new relationship with a great girl of his own. We are not saying that this is an easy thing to do. In some ways it might feel like a miniature breakup of its own. You might even find yourself surprised that you feel so worried about not having this person in your life, or worse, having him in your life with a shiny new girlfriend! But out of respect for the relationship you are cultivating, and for the sake of its healthy growth, you may have to do a little weeding.

Now, if you and your guy pal are genuinely just friends, maybe it is a matter of altering the dynamic between you. It isn't your fault that sitting on his lap has always been par for the course. And how about sharing a hotel room when you go with him on a road trip? Although these behaviors were once status quo, now they will only look rude to your significant other. The more you can help

HAVE *SEX* LIKE YOU **JUST** MET . . .

your man to see why your relationship with *him* is special and that his comfort level is very important to you, the closer you two can become. Then both of you can be friends with your friends but still understand the boundaries that both of you need to respect. If your friend can't appreciate the new rules you two must now follow in order to give your relationship its due respect, then maybe you need to reconsider that particular friendship. But if you guys truly are friends, we believe you won't have a problem.

Just like Susan: "Now, I am like the aunt of my ex-boyfriend and his now-wife's new baby. She really pushes our friendship. I think it's very healthy."

Can It Be Done? Five Examples of Platonic Male-Female Friendships

1. The Duck Man and Molly Ringwald
2. Lucy and Charlie Brown
3. Harry Potter and Hermione Granger
4. Calamity Jane and Wild Bill Hickok
5. The Little Mermaid and the Crab dude
   . . . Harry and Sally (well, not really)

No One Should Feel Like a Third Wheel

Five dates for you, your man, and a friend.

- *Movie and Dinner*: Go to an action movie and follow it up with dinner. Then all three of you have something in common to talk about so no one feels left out.
- *Sledding*: A winter sport where everyone's skill level matches can be a great way to bond and have a good time together.

- *Show off*: If you are going out with your guy friend and your man, do something that will make your man feel good about himself. Pick an activity at which he excels. If you are going out with him and his lady friend, choose something that you are good at and be polite about sharing it with her.
- *Double dates*: Set your guy friend or his gal friend up with another friend, and the four of you can all go out together. It is disarming for everyone. If a love connection ensues, you have new couple friends, which is a great bond for you and your guy.
- *Shopping*: Going furniture or food shopping isn't sexy, so having a third party there won't detract from the activity and will give everyone a chance to get to know each other in a place where defenses aren't up.

Fantasies and Crushes

It's a no-brainer: Some of the best sex is entirely in your head. "For me, the secret to having great sex is having a great imagination," says Tara. "My guy doesn't have know what I'm thinking about, but it certainly benefits him." Therefore, we don't want to take away your fantasies and crushes. What we want to do is help you to incorporate them into your relationship instead of separating them out. In other words, we understand your occasional need to imagine yourself in bed with the lead singer from (Insert Band Here), but we don't want you to actually insert the band, like there, if you know what we're saying.

Sometimes flirting with others can be a healthy way to remind yourself and your partner that you are desirable, which can be way sexy rather than way aggressive if you know how to play it. In other words, flirting, as long as you don't metaphorically fuck with each other, can lead to great, well, fucking. So, if your guy is jealous of his best friend for any reason that you know of, pick another target. As you flirt, at some point, mid-conversation, catch your man's eye and hold it. Then go back to flirting after having made it very clear (with your eyes, not like sign language) whom you will later be joining in the coatroom . . .

Flirting is best done with strangers and not coworkers, mutual friends, or your guy's brother. And then, it is even better if your man is in on it. Of course, it's harmless to smile extra wide at the cash register when ordering your deli sandwich. And there's nothing wrong with giggling a little louder on the phone at the joke of the guy with the sexy voice at the Chicago office. But what happens when the guy at the cash register asks for your number or sexy voice guy turns up at the spring convention?

"Everyone knows what too far means," says Kate. "You don't even have to have gone too far to realize you've gone too far. It's like Uzbekistan: Miles before you get there, you know you've left the country."

If you genuinely feel confused about what your partner might consider betrayal, it never hurts to ask. Use it as an opportunity to let him know what you think of the matter as well. This is another conversation we suggest you have in the most casual of places. Don't set it up with any serious expectation. And have it long before the issue is actually on the table. Bring it up over drinks or on a no-TV Tuesday. Start by saying something that he might mistake as complimentary like, "So, who flirted with you today?" The answer might lead to a great conversation, or if you let it, someplace much hotter.

Setting the Rules

After you are done having great sex, you can start the conversation about touchy subjects. "Choose your battles wisely," says Ostrofsky about laying down the law. "Identify what are deal-breakers, nice-to-haves, and off-the-radars or unimportant issues. This way, when you're upset about something, you have a set of categories for comparison."

Try to keep the conversation light and avoid feeling defensive. This works both ways. If he says that he hates the idea of you using the co-ed bathroom at your office, don't respond with a hot-headed "It isn't like we're wiping each other!" Instead, hear him out as though he is not criticizing you, your boss, or your boss's bathroom rules. He's just a guy telling you that he really likes you and here are some reasons that he knows he really likes you. (Mostly because they make him mad.) Then try to come up with compromises. Because you cannot change the rules of your office overnight, try to make him feel better about the situation by saying you will make a point of waiting until the bathroom is free of men before you use it. You can also let him know you'll bring it up with your boss.

The opposite is true too. When, for example, you hear that the last strip club he visited was last Wednesday, and he means of the past month and not of the past millennium, don't have a heart attack. This is the rules discussion, which means behaviors *prior* to the rules discussion don't count.

But what do you do with his strip club admission? And while we're at it, what do you think about strip clubs? Before you even go about setting up or down rules, take a minute to think about what you think of most legal sexual pastimes. If you aren't sure because you've never tried it, maybe one outcome of the rules discussion

HAVE **SEX** LIKE YOU **JUST** MET . . .

will include a porn sampler or a night at a strip club. Like Sasha, you might decide it's a fun thing to do every once in a while with your guy. "I planned a birthday party for my ex at a strip club," she says. "It was so funny because everyone was wasted and the strippers were hitting on the *girls*." Those ladies know how to disarm their female clientele. Who knows? You might have a good time and rediscover your libido!

The same goes for porn. It can't hurt to watch at least a part of one and see if anything happens. Think of it scientifically. We bet your guy will even be willing to do the legwork by offering up websites and movies you might enjoy. He'll probably even foot the bill and leave you alone for a private screening to see what you like. You might be surprised by all the different types of porn that are out there. (Check out Chapter 4 for tips on choosing and watching porn.) Amy says, "I think I watch it more often than he does. As long as the porn isn't degrading to women, I don't mind it." If you find something you like, suddenly you can incorporate it into your sex life, including trying the "Do whatever they're doing on the TV" game or "Make Your Own Porn," minus the camera crew. (Agree that you will both witness the tape being destroyed when the game is over!)

We caution you to know what rules you are making before locking them into place. In other words, before you prohibit porn from your man's sexual diet, make sure you've had a bite of the proverbial apple.

But there are times when one of you begins to overuse the sexual device of choice. "When does it become a problem?" asks Steinhart. Then she answers her own question: It's when the other thing gets chosen over your partner "time and time and time again." The best way to evaluate if you or your guy has a problem is to set the rules then see if they're kept.

Rachel says of a friend's ex, "He would come home late at night and change his underwear and go sleep in the other room. When she noticed what he was doing, my friend gave that guy a few stipulations if he wanted to stay together. One was no more strip clubs, and he couldn't do it."

We Asked. He Answered.

Q: *What would you do if you were betrayed while in a serious relationship?*

A: It's called "cheating" for a reason. I'm not the expert on this. Now, I would just get the fuck out. There's nothing to solve after a betrayal of trust. —HENRY

Not being able to stick to the rules can be more than a sign of disrespect toward you. It can also be a sign that your man needs help. In this case, ask him to talk to a professional about his compulsions. If he refuses, we hate to be Debbie Downers, but you might have to leave him to figure out for himself if he wants you or *Debbie Does Dallas*. And if he agrees, you still need to follow your heart as you wait beside him to watch him heal. Like any addict, recovery isn't easy and is often accompanied by setbacks. So, stick around if you want to, but pay attention to your needs and limits as you go. The best thing you can be for both of you is strong. And suggest that he seek the help of a professional. You can't "fix" him. (We go into this further in Chapter 10.)

Road Maps Back from Betrayal-Land

Sometimes intimacy and sexual problems can be a direct result of a betrayal. Whether or not rules had ever been verbally established, there are just those expectations we have, usually directly proportional to what we would or wouldn't do, that when broken can absolutely shake our personal foundations and lead us straight to the Ben and Jerry's for an indefinite amount of time. Lies and cheating are two major obstacles from which couples can have a hard time recovering.

Holly points out that she isn't even sure her man cheated on her. She explains, "It was linked to a huge lie that pretty much destroyed me."

For Sharon, a marketing manager in Toledo, Ohio: "It still hurts me to think about the guy who cheated on me, and I don't think I'll ever get over it."

Marie forgave her man for cheating at first but ultimately concluded, "You don't forget, so even though we tried to make it work, visions kept coming back into my head until eventually we broke up for good."

So is there hope for a relationship where there's been cheating? "Of course there is," says Steinhart, "if you want to be with this person. You have to tell yourself that you're with an imperfect human being. Ask yourself not only if you can trust them again, but also if you can love an imperfect person."

However, while recovering from a major betrayal is a hefty proposition, it isn't impossible. Take Amy who tells this story: "I know a couple who have been together since high school. The story was that, in college, he got drunk and slept with someone and then he told her that they had just kissed. When it came out that they had actually slept together, it seemed like a deal-breaker. But they worked it out. And now they have a second baby on the way."

The truth is that making a blanket assessment about whether or not to forgive men or women in general for cheating is like saying everyone with blue eyes should dye their hair blond. Some complexions just can't take it. And anyway, you know your relationship (and complexion) better than a self-help book does.

Liz, a bartender in Philadelphia, Pennsylvania, sums it up like this: "Sometimes people are just working their shit out. Relationships can be scary sometimes."

"The person who cheats might be hurting," says Steinhart. "And it's not about you. It's about them, their own insecurity, their own need to be loved their own way. So what can you offer?"

"It's not always just the cheater who is to blame," says Sasha. "I think I realized the first time that there was something wrong with my marriage when I found myself really attracted to someone else."

If the infidelity is due to a mutual dynamic that you believe you are both willing and able to change, then by all means, forgive and move on. Ultimately, we hope your relationship is not expendable. It at least deserves an honest assessment. Just because something is difficult doesn't mean it won't be incredibly satisfying once you figure out what both of you want and if you are both able to meet those wants. One thing we know for sure is this: Wanting to make each other happy is a staple of any healthy love affair. If you can't agree on that, maybe this relationship isn't ready to move forward.

Close the Open Book
(If You Want Him to Write in It)

This chapter has focused on communicating your expectation for your relationship and creating an honest and trusting environment. Once this trust is firmly in place, you will find it becomes much easier for both of you to begin opening up about your sexual desires.

Ostrofsky suggests that the best way to begin sharing your sexual desires with your guy is to start by knowing exactly what they are. "When you think before you speak," she suggests, "you are able to be honest with yourself about what you want and how he can give it to you." As for getting him to spill, she says this is also important. "It is likely he wants something too so open up this dialogue in and out of the bedroom."

But the best way to put the kibosh on your spanking new spankings is to start spilling the beans about it to everyone you know. We totally get it that our guys are in their proverbial locker rooms discussing information we would close our ears and hum to if they ever tried to set it in front of us. For example this, er, nugget from Nina really makes the point about the whole Mars and Venus thing: "While I was off telling my girlfriends where the best places were that I've ever been kissed by men and things like that, my boyfriend was discussing the shape of their girlfriends' boobs with his BFFs." So there it is. We all talk. Except our boob-shape conversation is more along the lines of the interpersonal while theirs are often just sort of inter-anatomical . . .

But this need to explore feelings and experiences with our friends can be a very important part of our lives. "I do talk to my close friends," says Laura, "And my best girlfriends hear it all.

They keep me on the straight and narrow as well. And are my best cheerleaders when I need it."

"I have friends that I'll blab to about our sex life, but not about our more loving, intimate moments," says Amanda. "I have friends I'll share fight details with. I have some friends to whom I'll spill it all."

When it is beneficial to your relationship—when it helps you sort out your ideas or organize your feelings on matters—open discussions with good, trustworthy friends are a must. Like Sharon who says, "I think women especially need to talk about relationships with their friends to get perspective, and to vent."

However, when the banter is more for the sake of gossip, it might be doing more harm to you and your relationship than good. "Sometimes," begins Vanessa, "you know how girls can be—we just like a good story. It's easy to get caught up in that."

For Renee, a television promotions manager in New York City, getting into a serious relationship changed some of the ways she talks to her friends about her sex life. "I have always been very open about everything," she says. "But now that I am in a real relationship, I find myself stopping myself from saying certain things. I am trying to be more conscious of how open I am because I know he doesn't think the whole world needs to know everything. And he's probably right!"

Sasha agrees, saying, "It's really not okay to talk about everything if it's a serious partner, but it's okay if it's a frivolous one."

It's important to be careful where and to whom you are sharing intimate details. Vanessa has a blog in which she talks about her relationship but she and her guy have this deal, "He gets to approve everything before I post."

As for Amanda, her Internet journal has also taken on a new look since her relationship became serious. "I used to be more 'public' about all matters, but have decided I need to pick and choose who can read what. It's only fair to him, and let's face it, me too."

Holly understands why it's important to check in with her friends. After all, she says, "I trust my girlfriends over *Cosmo*." But when it comes to her guy spilling their proverbial beans, Holly says, "If it's low key I don't mind but if he is bragging, I mind. I'm shy, and don't like 'others' to know my business."

We Asked. **They Answered.**

Q: How do you feel about your girlfriends talking with their girlfriends about your relationship? Is there anything you feel should be off-limits?

A: HENRY: No, you should be able to tell your friends everything, because we are telling our friends everything.

A: DAVID: I feel totally comfortable with her discussing anything with her girlfriends that she is willing to discuss with me as well. I would prefer to not be embarrassed by something she would reveal.

A: KYLE: I don't think any guy likes girls talking about stuff that happens in the sack. The deal with guys is that if you are in a serious relationship, you don't talk about sex stuff with your friends. It's only the Casanova-escapades that get attention like that among "the guys."

CHAPTER 4

TEACHING HIM . . .
AND
LETTING HIM
TEACH YOU

" I once drew a diagram of the female sexual reproductive system—kind of like the kind in health class—over drinks for a boyfriend in order to show him where the clitoris was located on a woman. He was horrified even though I waited until we were on, like, our third drink. We didn't have sex for a while after that. "

—Heidi, business manager, San Francisco

Put On Your Own Oxygen Mask Before Assisting Other Passengers

We've already mentioned the importance of learning your own body and what, how, and where it feels good. You cannot know too much. After all, how can you let your man in on what you want if you aren't even sure where you can go to get it?

Before we go one step further, you should know that even the ladies who think they know every inch of themselves probably have a thing or two to learn. And you'd be surprised how long it takes many women to learn anything at all about their bodies.

"When I was a sophomore in college, about ten girls—none of whom were virgins—were hanging out in a dorm room and the topic of orgasms came up," says Nina. "One girl asked, 'How do you know if you've had one?' and another girl said, 'Oh, you'd know. They're super awesome.' It turned out six out of ten had never had one! After that everyone got vibrators for their birthdays."

Okay, so what is an orgasm? What does it feel like? How can you know for sure if you've had one? And, if you're pretty sure you haven't, how do you have one?

Besides being "super awesome," an orgasm is physically a series of rhythmic contractions in muscles primarily of the pelvic region (but it contracts muscles elsewhere too, which is what that face-grimace thing you've seen is all about) resulting in a fabulous feeling and culminating in relaxation. In other words, an orgasm is a powerful force. The feeling itself varies from person to person, however a good description from June, a pilot in Burlington, Vermont, is: "It feels both violent *and* peaceful. Like being hit but not feeling pain."

Hetty, a sales rep in Buffalo, New York, says, "It's as if the feeling is rising and rising and finally peaks and then you ski down the mountain."

"The good ones will really curl your toes," says Diane, a store manager in Chicago.

Now, what can you do if you haven't had one? Should you simply call yourself "frigid" and put on a habit? We say, not yet.

The first thing to do may not be to run out and buy yourself a vibrator with a spinning head, however tempting that may be. In fact, that might put you off hardware for good. We also aren't the biggest proponents of dropping trow and sitting on the cold linoleum of the bathroom floor with a compact mirror for getting to, um, third base with yourself. Sure, you can look down there. Don't be afraid to take a gander. Just don't expect to get flowers from yourself afterward. That move is purely clinical and not at all sexy. Second, removing fabric from between your "special place" and the device you plan to use for "going at it" might also wind up leaving you in a yawn session or worse, traction. Underpants increase surface area and actually allow more room for "error" and increased pressure. Also it is way less scary for beginners. Okay, so leave on underpants (preferably, soft ones), check. No vibrator, check. Now what?

The very best way to find your orgasm is to figure out what turns you on. Try to remember the first time you felt something, anything down there. Was it while you were watching your mom's soap opera and saw two people kissing? Was it after rubbing up against something? Early sexual sensation often comes when we are young and feels quite natural until someone yells at us for touching our privates in public.

"When I was little," admits Gail, a researcher in Columbus, Ohio, "I got this ticklish sensation down there from watching World Wrestling Federation. I was like six! I totally didn't get it, but it made me rub myself. My mom had to tell me that I had to do that in the bedroom. So embarrassing."

Often, our early experiences with our own sexuality can feel embarrassing. It isn't usually that people mean to shame us out of our sexual urges, but more likely, it just freaks people out to come across it. As a culture we tend to marginalize our sexuality. We sometimes really don't know what to do about children who are learning their own sexuality.

"The first time I saw my little sister masturbating, she was seven and I was fourteen," says Kelly, an assistant in Omaha. "I told her what she was doing was gross and dirty. It made her cry. I still feel so bad about it."

Okay, so now that you have all these suppressed, mortifying memories, er, find some new ones, like the way you feel when your boyfriend kisses you or movie scenes with hot and heavy sex in bathroom stalls. Maybe play the music you love to make out to. Whatever it takes.

"Relax, relax, relax!" says Katy Zvolerin of Adam & Eve, a company that specializes in sensual products. She recommends starting with "a nice hot bath and a glass of wine. Accepting yourself and allowing yourself to explore what feels good shouldn't be so hard."

Now, we recommend lying on your back for easier access, but lying on your front and using something to rub against like a pillow works too. Now gently rub. You should feel something pleasant like a warm tingle start to build. If you start to feel bored, stop.

Start again later. The point is to begin to allow for a buildup of pleasure. If it just feels ho-hum, don't force it. (As a side note—if you feel pain when you put pressure on that area and lessening the pressure you are applying doesn't help, there could be something physical going on. You might want to make an appointment with your gynecologist and get it checked out.) As you go, listen to and learn to respond to your body. Take your time and go with what feels good. Allow your muscles to tense—maybe even try squeezing your butt and leg muscles. But even if your muscles are tense, your mind should be relaxed—let yourself go mentally. If you remain unsure whether you have reached orgasm, keep going. We bet when you finally do, you won't have a single question except, "Where'd that hot guy I'm dating say he was going again?"

And if you still don't get there, we give you permission to go ahead and try a vibrator. "I recommend starting off with something small and discreet, such as a pocket rocket or something from the Natural Contours line of massagers," says Zvolerin. "It's amazing how many women write in to Adam & Eve thanking us for helping give them their first orgasms."

As If There Were Enough Hours in a Day . . .

Why do guys seem to cum so much easier that women? Steinhart says, "Maybe it's because they have more practice. So the resolution is to practice." Here are some tips on finding time to masturbate:

- Leave work early, or better yet, take a sick day. Seriously play sick. When everyone asks how you're feeling the next day, you'll honestly be able to say, "A hundred times better!"

- Take advantage of your guy's business trips. Make sure you tell him how much you're missing him—what he doesn't know doesn't hurt!
- No one interesting to talk to at the party? Leave early. There are much more exciting things to do at home.
- There isn't anything better to do while you're watching any movie starring any of the last ten "Sexiest Man Alive" winners.
- Skip the housework this week. Scrub the toilet later. This will be much more enjoyable.
- Can't sleep? This will pass the time—and probably tucker you out.

The Man Who Thinks Girls Come Just by Looking at Him

Knowing what turns you on can be a little difficult to figure out. But knowing what *doesn't* turn you on? Or even turns you off? Well, that's much easier. Usually, you figure it out when you're, say, getting hot and heavy with him, totally in the mood, feeling like you're on your way to something pretty spectacular, when all of a sudden, he squeezes your breast and turns it like when those guys in middle school used to grab each other's nipples and do "titty twisters." Ouch. And just like that, the moment is lost.

So, he's a little clueless about what turns you on—or even about what it takes to get you off? It's hard to talk about this stuff, for a number of reasons. First off, you don't want to seem like you're totally picky, prissy, uneasy to please, or just plain bitchy. And, well, you don't want him to feel like less of a guy. Even though it may sound ludicrous, many men pride themselves on their sexual prowess, no matter how delusional they might be. It's important not to hurt his pride or his feelings. But it's also important to enjoy yourself.

Don't worry—you can work with this, like Tara did. "For the longest time, I think he thought that the harder he rubbed my 'parts,' the more I'd enjoy it," says Tara. "But what he didn't get is that it was a soft touch that made me go crazy. After a while, I had to start saying things like, 'Oooh, it feels best when you touch me really gently, just like that.' It worked. Lots of positive moaning helped quite a bit too."

Positive feedback goes a long way. "It's not critical or confrontational," points out Steinhart. Let's face it, guys have big egos, so a little stroking definitely helps more than telling him when he's doing something wrong. When he's doing something you like, don't be afraid to tell him you like it—and why it's so pleasurable. The more specific you can get, the better your results can be. Tell him to keep going or tell him to go faster or slower or harder or softer, all the while saying what a great job he's doing. Yes, it sounds a bit like training a puppy but believe us, it will work.

"I like to talk dirty," says Carla, a publicist in New Brunswick, New Jersey. "He'll do anything if I say it in the right way, which basically means I make him feel like a stallion."

Another strategy is the wordless approach. Some men don't like to talk. They like to act. And here's where the moaning comes in. Or physical clues. You don't like the position you're in? Switch it up. You can do this even if he's stronger than you—it usually takes just a little rolling or adjusting. Once he realizes you're trying to take control, we think he'll be okay with it and will let you manipulate the situation however you want.

You'd really like him to be touching your breasts right now? Take his hands and put them there. More specific clues? Move his hands or body (butt cheeks even) however you'd like them to be moving. This is a not-so-subtle hint. Be clear. But stop at forcing him to do anything—you wouldn't want him to do that to you either. We think that goes without saying but thought we'd say it anyhow.

Now, rewind to the foreplay. "He'd totally rush into the situation," Stephanie, a sales consultant in Atlanta, says. "Forget foreplay. It'd be three kisses, then he'd be rarin' to go. And I totally wasn't." In this kind of situation, you're not even close enough to being turned on to even *care* about teaching him, right, ladies? But you *have* to do something because, well, you care about your physical relationship, and you still want to feel connected to him as well, are we right?

Take some advice from Tara, who says, "He had sexual ADD. So I had to make it interesting for him. When he just couldn't wait to have sex, I made sure he was 'getting some' without going all the way. I'd touch his penis, and he'd keep kissing me and touching me for as long as I wanted. Or I'd go down on him— and then he'd be more likely to go down on me right afterward. Or at the same time even."

So you might have to make it worth his while to continue the foreplay, but in the end, it will definitely be worth your while. Most women say they're more likely to enjoy sex if they've had plenty of foreplay to start it off. And we want you to enjoy it as much as possible—um, that's pretty much why we wrote this book.

Getting Serious

We've talked about being physically ready for sex, but sometimes there are emotional issues that can get in the way of your sexual intimacy and satisfaction. We're talking issues that are seriously disrupting your sex life, not letting you enjoy it in a healthy, normal way. This includes a history of being forced into sex, a past sexual experience that was negative, or even an upbringing where sex was taught to be wrong or dirty. Or maybe it's something you don't quite understand or can't remember. Sex can be confusing, and these types of issues can be difficult to get past. Don't feel bad about them, but rather, be brave enough to try to deal with them.

If you haven't shared these issues with your lover, you might want to do so. If he has a better understanding your behavior, you may both be better equipped to work through the problem together.

"It takes time and it takes getting help," says Steinhart.

Seek therapy for deep-seeded problems that are interfering with your sexual connection with your guy.

Maren, a graphic designer in Long Island, New York, and her guy went to counseling for their relationship—her results were positive, and we think it can be for you too. "It did help. Lots," she says.

Sasha and her guy were having sexual issues, and she suggested therapy. "Our sex life was lacking," she says. "We only did it once a month, and when it did happen it was only five minutes of the same boring routine. I wanted to go to counseling, but he didn't, which didn't help an already failing relationship. It made me feel that he was putting his pride ahead of his love for me by not being open to it, like I wasn't worth working for." And isn't your relationship worth working for?

When it comes to getting past previous sexual abuse, "there's a book that can help called *The Courage to Heal*," says Steinhart. "It's fabulous. There's a workbook and then there is a book for the partner that the authors have developed, and it's very useful."

Maybe it's your guy who has sexual issues. If you notice from the beginning your guy has his own hang-ups, make sure you do not take it personally. We can't emphasize this enough. You don't want his issues to become yours. Kindly, compassionately suggest therapy—either just for him or for the two of you together. Explain to him that you want to be with him, and that you're willing to help him through the problem.

If your guy refuses to seek help, you may want to schedule your own appointment with a counselor for your own mental stability. And don't be afraid to discover that, until your partner is ready to look seriously at his own issues, you might not be able to keep the relationship going. You cannot change him—and you can't let his problems hurt your own mental and sexual health.

Why It's Harder to Enjoy Yourself Now Than It Was in the Beginning

With many couples, the story goes the same way. You meet. You like each other. You can't keep your hands off each other. Wearing underwear becomes a foreign concept to you, and the lifetime supply of condoms he bought at Costco dwindles. Then, one day, you wake up, roll over, and look into his smoldering eyes and all you can think is, "I hope he makes this quick, so I don't have to deal with his morning breath for long." Where did the passion go?

"When you can have sex anytime you want, it can become a commodity," says Ostrofsky. One that you can start to take for granted.

When the passion fizzles, sex can become perfunctory. You stop trying new things, and even sometimes stop doing the really, really fun things.

"We go down on each other less now than we did when we were first dating," says Carla. "In general, there's less sense of adventure in our act these days."

Listen, just because Harrison Ford got a little older didn't mean that his stunt scenes in the last Indiana Jones got all crotchety. The old man can kick some ass. And your not-so-new sexual relationship can too.

Take the all-too-common scenario: Mr. Morning Breath is all over you. You start going at it. You start to do that flick-of-your-hip. You know, that move that will get you from zero to blast-off before you know it. No sense in beating around the bush; it's all about "the big O," right?

"It kind of *is* about the O for me," says Melissa W.

Hey, it's okay to want to come. But the problem with using the quickest trick to get the orgasm is that it becomes the *only* focus of your lovemaking—which makes it nothing like lovemaking. Plus, this is the chapter about learning and teaching, and no one's learning anything if you're only using the same moves over and over.

You're going to have to refocus your mindset. Sex should be more about general pleasure and less about a show-stopping climax (even though one is *fantastic*).

"It's not only about the big O," says Carrie, who works in investment banking in New York City. "Just being intimate and having that connection is enough."

The same goes for Maren: "Sex for me is about enjoying being close to my guy, feeling his warmth, his entire body."

As you're making love, make a mental note of the things you're enjoying. Take deep breaths. Really *feel* his skin with your fingertips—and whatever else is touching him too. Touch yourself. Enjoy yourself. Live in the moment, damn it!

We know, we know. That can be the biggest problem of all: *Letting* yourself enjoy it. "Sometimes my mind wanders," says Holly. And for whatever reason, that also becomes more noticeable as the relationship lengthens. There's lots of info on how to deal with that in Chapter 5. For now, we've got some more reasons to at least try to love sex for more than just the climax:

"The before and after are even better than an orgasm because that can last as long as we want," says Maren.

Sharon agrees: "For me, it is about being able to be as close to my partner as possible and to be intimate."

Plus, well, we've found that the more you find yourself trying to get to the orgasm, the less likely you are to have one.

The Elusive Orgasm

You're not coming? Don't think you're alone. According to Health. com, only one in four women regularly experiences an orgasm during intercourse. One-third of women report that they rarely or never do. If you don't either, you totally shouldn't give up—you can have one! However, you can enjoy yourself even when you don't reach the summit.

"I don't tend to reach 'the big O' during intercourse," says Rachel. "But I do from oral sex. I don't think that it matters if a woman orgasms from sex, as long as it feels good and she's enjoying it."

"Don't feel like you can't ask to be finished off if you didn't come," advises Amy. Right on, Amy! If oral sex is what makes you come, ask him to do a little follow-up cunnilingus. Like vibrators? Maybe he'll be willing to use one on you—before *or* after his big "O." Or, maybe he's willing to try a little "sex enhancer" toy like the Durex Play Vibrations Vibrating Ring. It's a little ring he can put over his jammy to make it—you guessed it—vibrate. And for whatever reason, things that vibrate loosen our muscles and sometimes our minds. Plus, they feel damned good, and therefore, are more likely to make women come. Oh, and we've got lots more sex toy recommendations in Chapter 8, so keep reading!

Trying everything and still not coming? Don't get discouraged. "If you expect to have mind-blowing sex each time, you will only be disappointed," says Holly. She takes her nonorgasmic sexual moments with a grain of salt: "Sometimes it just so happens that I don't." And that's that.

"I always come because if all else fails, I do it myself," adds Vanessa. That's okay too. Guys are usually very supportive when women take matters into their own, um, hands.

Amy reiterates Rachel's sentiment: "I think as long as you are having sex because you want to, you enjoy the guy, and it feels good, it should be okay if you don't come."

The Dos and Don'ts of Foreplay

Sex is a two-way street. If you're both into it, it can be a wonderful, amazing experience for both of you. But if *he's* not into it, it can be miserable for you too. So, encouraging him to be in the right mood for a romp in the hay can be as simple as following a few do's and don'ts.

Do be positive. A big mistake is to start a sexual prelude with a list of ways he could improve in the bedroom. That would be like him running down for you all the body parts that he thinks could use a little toning and then expecting you to feel hot—you wouldn't, right? Instead, try using physical cues like saying, "Do to me whatever I do to you." Then proceed to increase and decrease speed and pressure at your discretion. It can be very erotic.

Do respect him—and show it. "Pay attention to how you are treating him outside the bedroom," says Sasha. "You aren't going to be attracted to someone whom you are treating like your child in the rest of your life." And unless he has a total Oedipus complex, we're guessing that he's going to be turned on less the more you act like "Mom."

Don't run home from a late night at the office, tear off your coat and yell, "I've got ten minutes before *Dancing with the Stars*, let's do this thing!" Make time for sex—by *time*, we mean one without a kitchen timer dinging to signal the end of it. Sex should be a priority in your life, not something you race to get over with.

Don't eat a really heavy dinner on a night you hope to do it. A big burger and fries is only going to leave you in a bloated food coma. Instead, order out for sushi or make a big salad. Try throwing in a few aphrodisiacs like oysters and cranberries. For dessert, forget the plates and eat it off each other.

Don't use drama as a means to creating passion. It might seem like starting an argument for no reason at all can keeps things exciting, but it can weaken the overall structure of the relationship. "Drama adds problems, and I have never found it to be passionate —just stressful," says Carrie. It's like Magneto in the *X-Men*. He can use his power to mutate the world, but the strain it puts on his body will kill him.

Sexy Teacher Outfits . . . on the TV Screen

Looking for another learning tool? Instructions for how to give the perfect blow-job? Ideas to bring into the bedroom? Some couples turn to pornography to satisfy those urges. And we totally think you should give it a shot, at least once. You may benefit more from it than you thought.

"I use porn to see if I can pick up tips to add to my repertoire," says Laura. That's right, you could learn a new position—reverse cowgirl anyone?—or another new sexy move. It could also make you learn to adopt new attitudes toward sex with your guy. But the things you learn from a naughty movie could go so much . . . er . . . deeper.

For starters, you could learn to let go a bit. "For us, it makes us kind of loosen up about sex," says Alexandra, an editor in Boston. Watching even the most far-fetched porn can turn you on and help you and your guy both lose inhibitions. Remember that just because you're watching other people do it doesn't mean you're thinking about those other people. It just means you're thinking about sex. And it might make you think about it in a new, fresh, less buttoned-up way.

While you're watching the porn movie, try talking about it a little. The more sexy, dirty talk (and the less clinical), the better. When the "actors" are performing certain moves—especially the ones that turn *you* on—ask him if he likes them. And tell him what you like. "It can help with communicating what each partner wants from the other," says Sasha. And, if you feel so inclined, try it out. Make out with him while you're watching; we think it will lead to some very hot lovemaking. You both may open up about feelings you've never known how to express before.

"I think the best thing porn can do is get you turned on and creative. If a certain situation or position excited you a lot, try re-enacting it by role-playing," says Amy. "A lot of a healthy sex life is an open mind, I think."

If you let your guy choose the video—maybe it's one that he secretly watches when he's alone—you might learn even more about what turns him on. These are things he might not be comfortable expressing in words, or maybe he just doesn't know how to articulate them. Let's say he likes porn where the "plots" include spontaneous sex in unusual places. Doesn't that give you a little bit of a hint as to what is erotic to him? What about the way the women behave in the video? If they're treating the men like sex gods, maybe you could give *your* guy a little bit of extra praise in the sack. Use the porn as inspiration for ways you can naughtily flirt with him—and how you can approach him sexually.

If you're choosing a porno together, look for something on which you both can agree. Steinhart recommends checking out movies by Femme Productions. This is the brainchild of female adult filmmaker Candida Royalle, whose main focus is "couples erotica." "She's amazing, gorgeous, and accessible," says Steinhart.

For every couple, what works will be different, but here are some recommendations for *finding* what works that have proved effective for these women:

"Something that doesn't disrespect or disgust either party," says Carrie.

"I prefer soft-core movies with sensual sex scenes," says Holly.

"We have rented them from On Demand," says Alexandra. "I do know that if they have a really out-there title I'm probably going to get uncomfortable so I would never pick one of those. Regular old porn—as opposed to 'Asian Anal' or other fetish-type stuff—is usually wild enough for me!"

"What works is such an individual thing," says Maren.

These women are right to approach their choice of movies cautiously, at least at first. One or both of you might begin to feel uncomfortable if there are scenes that are degrading or involve some sort of strange fetish. You two must agree on the subject matter before popping the DVD into the player, and agree to hit eject if one of you starts to feel bothered.

So, we know the reservations you might have about skin flicks. They can be pretty absurd, right?

"I once saw one that involved a man in a giant lobster costume sneaking in windows to women's bedrooms," says Amy. "I believe he was called 'The Lobster Monster.'"

"I can't watch porn. The bad acting and over-acting—the moans and screams," says Holly. "It makes me laugh."

Sure, these films can be pretty hilarious or absurd. Sometimes that can interfere with you getting turned on—but the right movie can actually help.

"Laughing about it together is a way to be intimate," says Carrie. "You're sharing the secret of having watched it."

"I could *never* watch a porn without laughing a bit, so it kind of makes sex a sillier experience—which I think can be a good thing," says Alexandra. "Having a sense of humor allows me to loosen up and prevents me from thinking about whether I've waxed in the recent past or if my stomach looks fat when I move a certain way."

Amy agrees: "Porn can lighten the mood," she says. "You can laugh about it together while still being aroused and then you can channel that energy onto each other."

And, maybe you want do a little of your own "editing." "If you don't like the dialogue, turn the sound off," suggests Steinhart.

But what about those *people* in the movies? Women with perfect, cellulite-free thighs; breasts pumped up with silicone; and lips plumped up with collagen. Maybe you can't help but wonder if your guy is comparing you to them. Sasha puts it best: "It can make you feel inferior in the hot bod department."

But really do some thinking about this. Your guy is with *you*, not some sleazy-looking chick with bad hair extensions. Sure, he'll see that girl on the screen, but he *wants* you. I mean, we think James Franco is pretty hot, but we wouldn't leave our guys in a million years for him (umm . . .). It's a fantasy, a means to turning yourselves on, a way to sample a particular move or attitude without actually having to try it—you see it first on the screen and *then* decide whether it's right for you. And the reason he's so damned turned on while watching it is because he's thinking about having sex with you at the same time.

Also, take a look at the guys in the porn. Some of them look like Zeus; others, like an everyday Joe. Okay, now take a look at their cocks. Yes, their very, very large, unrealistic cocks. Is your guy with his normal, everyday-looking penis afraid to watch porn? Is he comparing his Johnson to theirs and getting all insecure about it? We didn't think so. Take a nod from him and learn to take the silicone and collagen with a grain of salt.

So, we say, with all these potential benefits, why not give porn a shot? You might find it really helpful. Of course, you might not. "It didn't do much for either of us," says Sharon. "We watched a video once, and even though we own it, we've never incorporated it again."

That's okay too. The point we want to make is that porn comes in all shapes and sizes and is *created* to be sexy. The lighting, the boom-cha-ka music, and the positions are all designed in a formula that for some people just triggers all the right things. If it doesn't work for you and your guy, try something else. Maybe you need a movie with a different style, story, or tone. Maybe you'd rather read a little erotica and look at pictures. Or maybe you need your guy to watch the porn by himself and whisper the plot line in your ear later that night when the clothes start coming off. Just figure out what works best for you.

CHAPTER 5

WHEN THE *DAY-TO-DAY* GETS *IN THE WAY*

> Over the holidays, our sex life definitely suffered. We were so exhausted from decorating the apartment for Christmas, shopping for gifts, going to parties, and all the other crap that comes along with the holidays that when we got home, all we wanted to do was go to sleep. Forget romance.

—Alexandra

Your Own Private Island

You've got a big report due tomorrow at work. Your grandpa has major surgery next week. And the baby's been crying all night. Um, sexy? We don't think so. And neither, we guess, do you. But here you are in your real life, and the fact is it's difficult to become a vixen in black leather after spending the day getting reamed out by your boss or getting puked on by your kid who has the flu for the second time this month. Even the dog's weepy "take me for a walk" face means less time for sexy, more time for picking up shit. In all this, it can be difficult to find your inner sex kitten. So what do you do?

Steinhart suggests, "Don't forget that there's this little oasis where you can be sexual with someone else, and that can be affirming." We are particularly taken with this nugget of wisdom. The idea that your relationship with your guy can be spiritually, emotionally, and psychologically transformed into a quiet place of safety, calm, and, sure, sex, is a pretty bad-ass suggestion. It's where you escape the stresses of life together. We imagine that if you suggested it to him, he'd agree.

"When I told my boyfriend that I wanted us both to use our relationship as a landing strip for the insanity in our lives, he thought it sounded awesome," says Vanessa. We know you're thinking, what guy wouldn't? To the male of our species, this might actually seem like a no-brainer. After all, this is the same guy whose eyes never leave the TV during a Browns game even when the living room is on fire. Women, who are sometimes accused of being the more emotional gender, might find it harder to compartmentalize. Work crisis equals crying well past dinnertime and does not make for a happy libido as the full moon lights the night sky. We do not deny that our argument is a sound one: Something explodes, we step away from the *Top Model* marathon, period. But imagine if you *were* able to leave work at work, the kids in the kids' room, and Fluffy the Rabbit's pellet wars in his cage until morning. But how?

"Sometimes," agrees Steinhart, "stress can push the libido way down."

If the stressor is specific and temporary, like there is a minor grease fire igniting on the stove, it's okay to say no that night when your man's hand starts its crawl up your leg. However, if the stressor is related to the construction that recently began across the street with a banner reading "Arriving in 2018!" splayed across its scaffolding, you might have to develop a new relationship to your libido and stress.

The good news is that stress can be good for your sex drive. "Sometimes stress can push your libido way up," Steinhart says. "Sometimes all people want is a sexual outlet."

We don't want to encourage you to *use* your man for sex and thus stress relief. (Is that him in the background yelling, "S'okay! Tell her it's okay to use me!"?) But we want to suggest that you find a way to remember that sex and exercise are sometimes one and the same. Even Dr. Kilpatrick says so: "Sex is sometimes a workout!" And workouts lead to a release of endorphins and other mood enhancers like adrenaline, as mentioned earlier by Dr. Altobelli. Since you already know that exercise is a great way to calm frayed nerves, perhaps sex can become a way for you to let loose and calm down. Like we said, this is your oasis with your man. And this oasis is sexy, like *Blue Lagoon*, Brooke-Shields-and-the-hot-blond-guy sexy. The water is sapphire, the air is warm, and you are young, naked, and curious. Don't worry—you have a better vocabulary, and your furniture is not all wicker.

"The tragedy is when you've got sex in the head instead of down where it belongs."

—D. H. Lawrence

Fold Laundry, Do It, Write Dissertation, Walk Snuggles

Perhaps it seems like there aren't enough hours in the day to brush your teeth (you *do* brush your teeth, we hope—if not, try it—we may have just solved your problem right there!), much less take it off, lube it up, and get it on. But it is up to you to find them. Steinhart says that, in her experience, a couple loses their mojo when they leave sex off their list of things to do. "It has to do with being lower on each other's priority list," she points out. "Work is more important. Sleep is more important. Committees are more important. Commitments are more important."

We recommend that you start making time for sex. We don't mean just saying, "I'm going to make time for sex from now on." A statement like this will go the way of last year's New Year's resolutions. Instead, physically take out your calendar, Blackberry, or planner, and schedule in sex. The first time around, you don't even need to discuss it with your man. Maybe you will discover that by simply making it something you intend to do, it will begin to happen more and more often. Of course, you may eventually have to coordinate your schedule with your guy so that you can both make the "appointment." This might sound a bit contrived—and therefore unsexy—but really you're showing each other that your sex life is a priority. You're both putting everything aside at exactly the same time. "OMG," writes Laura of her marriage that has spanned decades, "four kids, seven grandkids, countless animals in our life, two professional careers, you bet it can distract you. Scheduling time for each other, as you would schedule a meeting, is what got us through this. My husband would actually book a date in my scheduler, just like an evening meeting."

Imagine how special sex will seem if it becomes an event in your life to look forward to, something you both empower with supreme importance. Just make sure you write it in pink with hearts and smiley faces and not beside an ominous picture of the Jolly Roger—unless you like that sort of thing.

"I had heard that a pastor in Florida was recommending that married couples in his congregation try having sex every day for thirty days," says Yasmine, a writer in New York City. "So my husband and I tried it out. It was really tough in the beginning. We had to really plan out our days so we'd have enough time to do it before we got too tired at night—we were even having sex right after work or on weekend afternoons, which was fun! I admit that some days, we ended up not doing it, but by the end of the month, we were on a roll and we felt really close to each other! It was like we'd forgotten to make time for each other and we relearned how."

"It's amazing how once you start having sex—and enjoying it— you want to do it more and more," says expert Zvolerin.

Frequency of your scheduled romps should be something the two of you agree on. This is an important point. If you over-schedule yourselves, you might begin missing dates. In this case, the importance of the meetings diminishes, until they again become words on a page, and even worse, they become optional. Perhaps begin by only putting sex on the books once a month. Once that becomes regular, add a second sex date.

If you can do so, by all means, supplement your sexual encounters with "off the book" trysts, but this way, you slowly build until you know you and your man will take the sex appointments seriously. Then put as many on those to-do lists as you can fit. Of course, if it is Sunday the 7th after *60 Minutes* and the story about the refugee camp pretty much made the mood about as sexy as, well, a refugee camp, don't chuck chins with a "Maybe next time." Instead, use the time to cuddle. Have a conversation about your favorite part of each other's bodies. Look into each other's eyes. Make this time about cultivating the intimacy between the two of you.

Remember that when you and your guy are in the bedroom together, you are in a stress-free zone. This is the one place you should feel comfortable letting everything else go. "Make a decision to be here right now," says Steinhart. "Say to yourself, 'Forget about the laundry. Forget about the report due.' Say, 'This is where I am now. This is where I want to be.'"

When you're at the nursing home with your senile grandmother, be a dutiful granddaughter. In the kitchen making cookies with the kids, be Mommy. At work, be career-driven. But with your man, remember you are something more than his workaholic girlfriend or his shit-wiping honey, you are each other's lovers. You are each other's love machines. Each other's hot time in the city. And so forth. So act like it.

We bet your man will follow your cues naturally. And if he doesn't, let him in on your intention. See if he'll try it. Then set boundaries for it. In other words, be parents together, co-own your goldfish, complain about work and money issues during family time. But leave room for someplace amazing, someplace wonderful, without even leaving your house.

Let's Call It "Club Sexy"

No one expects you to run out and buy matching T-shirts with the name "Tigers" splashed across the chest. But we'd like you to take a minute and think about the two of you as members of an exclusive club. When a club meeting is called to order, rules must be followed:

- No cell phones.
- No criticisms or insults.
- Compliment each other at the beginning and end of the meeting.
- No discussion of children, pets, or work.
- No granny panties, flannel PJs, or farting (well, at least until *after* you do it).

We hope you and your man will take some time to figure out additional rules for the club. These rules can either be written down and unfurled like a pair of crotchless fishnets at the beginning of each meeting, or simply understood by both members of the club if say, one or both members of the club wish we weren't making you do this. However, in this way, you begin to build a trust with each other as more than just the everyday roles that you've been watching since your childhood. In this club, whether you designate a sexy space and time, or simply adopt a new behavior to your daily routine, you grow togther both sexually and sensually. You are promising each other to make meeting the other's physical needs as important a part of your lives as monetary and emotional needs.

Club Sexy is simply a way to consider your sexual selves as a unit—all hot, sweaty, and worn out in a good way. No, you don't have to call it that. But as a way to consider it, a club of two with rules and expectations, you might find it can be the thing that started funny, then got very very dirty.

While most clubs have rules, some also have clubhouses. But wait. Before you run and get your hammer and nails and start climbing the nearest burly oak, we'll let you use your bedroom for this one.

So, assuming your bedroom is your Clubhouse of Sex, let's take a minute to make sure it is appropriately decorated. And, no, we're not saying that you need silk sheets, a black velvet canopy, a vibrating bed, a stripper pole, or a mirrored ceiling (although, none of those would necessarily hurt). We're just saying that you need to edit out the stuff that makes it un-sexy. Now, the nice thing about men is that most of them are still internally just about eleven years old. This project, we suspect, will go over like gangbusters if you don't start by handing him a bolt of pink chiffon or a glue gun. Definitely hand him a power tool. Trust us. Hot guy with power tool equals win-win.

Now take a look around. What do you see? A picture of Grandma Tilly at the family picnic last summer framed on your desk? Aw, how sweet. What else? Oh, a computer in the corner with "You Have Mail" blinking in the corner, a telephone by the head of the bed, a PlayStation on the TV stand, your unmade bed, and no lock on the door. Okee-dokee. Now maybe we haven't accurately identified your bedroom, but maybe we got one or two pieces of it spot on. But no matter how you look at it, would you say that your bedroom is the perfect clubhouse for the Sinful Bear Club? We didn't think so.

The solution? "Remove the things that distract you," says Steinhart.

We recommend you start with the things that are easy. Take down photographs of all things unsexy. The photos of impoverished kids that you took on your year abroad in India can be moved to the hallway wall. The photographs of your nieces in tutus? Living room. Dad at your brother's wedding? Office.

You will be amazed by how different things feel once your relatives aren't watching. But don't stop there: Remove *all* distractions.

Unplug the TV. In fact, get rid of it all together. There's no reason Dave Letterman should be more appealing to you than your own guy as the clock approaches midnight. If this is a nonnegotiable, throw something over the TV for a few hours a night, like a red scarf or a tapestry. If you need to keep a TV in the bedroom, enlist it in the fight for the cause of the club. Make Thursday night sexy movie night. If porn isn't your thing, there is plenty of cinematic eye-candy out there that will enrich your mind and embolden your bod.

Make the room a no-communication-with-the-outside-world zone. Cell phones, pagers, laptops, and computers of all kinds should be left at the door or turned off before entering. Books are okay, but stay away from grad-school textbooks and biographies of anyone who died of an O.D.—unless they were mid-orgy. Opt instead for romance novels with Fabio-types drawn on the front cover or *The Kama Sutra*. If you are a read-to-sleeper, make a rule not to pick up your personal reading until you and your sweetie have read a few pages out of a book that the two of you agree upon. Reading out loud can be incredibly bonding and, depending on the material, incredibly hot. Of course, reading together quietly works too, if doing it out loud reminds either of you of being called out during eighth-grade English.

As for décor, the women we asked had a lot of great ideas for ways to make your room as hot as the Sahara on a summer afternoon.

"Turn off all overhead lighting. It's just depressing," says Simona. "Use a bedside lamp instead. If you find that glow is too strong and distracting, modify it with a sheer red scarf." It's amazing what a little mood-lighting can make or break.

Roxie suggests changing the smell of things. She says, "Patchouli incense if you are under twenty, an Urban Outfitters candle if you are twenty to twenty-nine, and an Anthropologie candle if you are over thirty." She also recommends moving in a stereo. "Electronica music if you want to make it obvious," she says. "Enigma album if you want to make it ridiculous, Biggie if you want to make it ghetto fabulous, and Justin Timberlake if you need to indulge your own rich inner fantasy life."

Toby's color scheme says a lot about her room. "It is decorated in rich velvet, deep reds, and creamy golds," she says. "I think my bedroom looks like a romantic cave." She also advises about the lighting scheme saying, "Mood-lighting with a dimmer is a plus too."

Courtney suggests "a clean and uncluttered space" to help put you in the mood. While Abby, a writer in Brooklyn, New York, thinks that candles are the key to going from sleepy to sexy. And

Eleanor, a botanist in New York City, says definitively, "No stuffed animals!"

Extreme Makeover, Bedroom Edition
Interior Designer Malee Ackerman of San Francisco, California shares tips for how to sexify your clubhouse.

- *When it comes to decorating a bedroom, it might be cliché to talk about painting your walls red—almost too 'in your face.' Instead, go for neutral colors like creams, beiges, and browns. These colors can be subtly sexy, especially when you add accents like silver throw pillows to add a little glitz.*
- *Speaking of accent pillows, there is such a thing as too many. You want your bed to be accessible and comfortable. And having too many pillows to unload before you can find your bed does not add to spontaneity at all!*
- *If you need a place to hide private items, especially ones you may not want your parents, kids, or house-sitters getting suspicious about, get a pretty jewelry box with a lock on it. Then take out the inserts! You'll be amazed at how much you can fit in there, how easily it sits on your bedside table, and how harmless it looks sitting there innocently.*
- *Make sure your bed is far enough away from the wall that it isn't banging up against it. Often this is the source of a lot of unwanted noises.*
- *If you have wood floors, floor grips might not be enough to keep your bed in one place. Get a gripping floor pad and put a carpet over it; then set your bed up on top of that to cut down on bed movement and noise.*

- *Windows are a good place to add accent colors. Warm, sexy colors like burgundy and gold add sensuous for little pops of color. Heavy drapery on windows block light and add a beautiful softness to the room. It's amazing how drapery adds that finishing touch. Alternatively, wood blinds are super crisp and clean and can add a great detail.*
- *Make the bed a central point in the room. This can be accomplished in a few ways. Try framing the bed with bedside tables that each have lamps and soft lampshades. These can draw the eye to the bed. Or you can elevate it with risers you can buy at Target and other stores—if your man is handy, have him take care of this.*
- *Artwork is a great way to personalize your space. Hang photographs that remind you of favorite places you've been together or places you want to go together. With digital photography, now it's easy to have your own images blown up on canvases and framed."*

Members Only

Remember that distractions also include children and pets. Fido and Suzy Jr. are not invited to Club Sexy. However, we know this can be a particularly difficult situation. You love them—they're adorable. Kids have nightmares and find your bed much cozier than their own—and they're so sweet and cuddly when they're asleep. Dogs bark and/or cry when the door is closed to them, and blasting Marvin Gaye over their wails is kind of abusive, no matter how bad you want some. We know there are certain times you have to make exceptions, but in general, it is important for the kids and pets to know their boundaries. Sometimes Mommy and Daddy need a little alone time. "Put a lock on your door," says Steinhart. This is not to be cruel, but rather to protect them from having to tell their therapist the story of the fateful day they barged in and found Mommy in her pasties and chaps. In order to have intimacy—and feel completely liberated—you and your guy must have some privacy. If you are already in a routine where you have little feet or little paws in your bed on a nightly basis, you have our permission to take this slow. Just know that sparks won't fly when you have living, breathing distractions in your bed with you.

Some people, however, find ways to keep their kids in bed with them and still maintain a healthy sex life without the kids around. There is a loud and thriving debate on this issue, and we respect your view, wherever you and your family falls. Julie, a homemaker in Williamstown, Massachusetts, says, "Sleeping and having sex are two different things. If one of the kids falls asleep in our bed, we use a bed in another room. Or we have sex when they are at school or napping." For Julie, sleeping with her children allows for a great closeness with them that would be otherwise impossible, but she agrees that it is important to make time for an intimate, private relationship with your partner. "In terms of establishing boundaries, they are certainly important in many areas of life," she points out. "But, we have not felt that we needed to keep the kids out when it comes to bedtime."

If the problem is a pet that will bark itself silly in the other room, it's okay to put it in its crate or on an adjacent dog bed while doing the deed, as long as you are not distracted. We have it on good authority that they will not tell anyone in the dog park what they witnessed.

"We finally got our dog on a dog bed, and she'll stay there until about 4:00 A.M., then she crawls in with us," explains Vanessa. "So we get the best of both worlds. We fall asleep with the two of us and then get to have our dog snuggle up during the night."

We want to encourage you to keep your bedroom the bedroom. Don't make it a regular meeting place for family and friends. Watch TV together as a family in the living room. Have an office in another part of the house. Eat dinner at a table in the kitchen, dining room, or television tray. If your kids now do their homework or watch TV on your bed, reorganize so that those things happen in another part of the house.

If you live in a studio and find yourself entertaining in what is basically your bedroom, try to implement items like Shoji screens and shelving units that will help you delineate a bedroom space. If your bed is a fold-out couch or a futon, put away a special blanket when you wake up that you only take out and add to your bed at night. Change the lighting and add some sensual music to make your space a clubhouse at the end of the day.

Eventually, the room will become the clubhouse of your dreams replete with tender whispers of "Pass the vibrator, please!"

We Asked. **He Answered.**

Q: *Have you ever dated someone who was good at explaining to you what she wanted in bed? What did she do or not do?*

A: I dated an older woman for a while in my late twenties. She was very honest and open about what she liked. And I feel it only enhanced our sexual relationship.—DAVID

The Flirtation Situation

You've already reeled in the guy, so the hook doesn't need to be baited anymore, right? Well, wrong. Couples in relationships that have stood the test of time will emphasize this, too: you need to flirt, no matter how long you've been together. Flirting can add excitement, romance, and, well, horniness. The hornier you are, the more you'll let loose in bed, eh? Never underestimate the power of flirting. And this doesn't mean just using all those tried-and-true pet names—it means trying new tactics, too.

Go ahead and start slowly. Touch his arm. Go on. Touch it. And toss back your hair and laugh while you're at it. See if it doesn't disarm him like a soldier at a puppy convention!

Courtney has similar, simple advice. "Just while you're sitting and watching TV, touch his leg," she says. "Take his head in your hands and kiss him. Sometimes just doing the thing can lead to *wanting* to do the thing."

Flirting means "sending him sweet, sexy texts in the middle of his workday, telling him what I'm not wearing. Smiling at him a lot in my sheepish sexy way," says Holly.

"If we're watching *Top Chef*, and I look over at my boyfriend and think, 'Damn, he looks hot right now,' I either tell him or pounce on him," says Alexandra.

But proceed carefully with this tactic. "Now if he's watching football and she starts kissing him, how responsive is he going to be?" asks Steinhart. "Not very. She has to make some choices too. She has to respect his needs."

Still, reminding your guy that you want him without actually having sex with him is a phenomenal way to begin reminding not just him but you about the sexual woman that lurks behind the stressed out executive assistant with the electric socket hair trying to fish a decent-looking blouse from the dirty laundry hamper.

Alexandra adds, "Grabbing his hand while we're sitting on the couch, grabbing his butt—or, I must admit, his package—when he's cooking dinner, giving him flirty eyes when we're out with friends. I think all of that goes a long way to making him feel like you still want him."

And making him feel wanted might lead to an actual physical connection. If you slather him with compliments like, "Great hands" or "Love how you look in that color," put the words in the throaty part of your voice where you are almost delivering the information in a purr. If the kids are in the room, sidle up and put them right in his ear. If your man has gone from the one you want to see as sexy to the one you wish would just fold the laundry for once, tune in to your body to see how it reacts to his touch or his appreciative glances.

Notice your man, and invite him to notice you again. Even if you guys have grown fat and happy together, find the steamy in the way he whispers your name or the colors in his eyes. It's there, even if you have to look for it.

Humor can also help lighten the mood enough to get you both turned on. "I usually make silly jokes to get him to laugh," says Amy. "Especially ridiculous sex puns, like if someone on TV says something like 'When are you coming over?' I'll lean on him and go, 'When are you coming . . . all over me?'

Amy also gets up and works it. "I 'strut' as he calls it," she says, "where I walk, stand, sit, lie or move a certain way so that he notices my boobs or ass."

Yes, this is a guy. He is a visual creature. Wear something excellent, even if you have no plans to leave the house. Don't let him come home to you with your hair in curlers. Yes, we agree that once he's fallen for you, he should love you even when you're wearing curlers—or that huge Care Bear tee shirt you bought in 1988. Chances are, he will. But will you? See what happens when you chuck Tenderheart Bear in the laundry (or hell, the trash) and jump in the shower. Then, throw something on that makes you feel hot and will definitely get you noticed. It isn't only him that will get a—rise—out of it, but you will too. *Feeling* sexy, after all is often synonymous with *being* sexy.

"I like to put on a sexy dress, high heels, and makeup on an unexpected night," says Sharon.

Laura avoids wearing granny panties. "I always wear very sexy lingerie—even to work," she says. "When I get home, I ask him to come in to tell me about his day while I change out of my clothes. He gets to watch the 'show' while we catch up. By the end, he always wants to help me 'get more comfortable.'"

Sarah Stark, coauthor of *The Lingerie Handbook*, agrees with Laura's tactic. "Don't get so comfortable with your significant other that he only sees you in saggy, baggy, stretched-out undies and dingy old bras," says Stark. "You shouldn't even be wearing those! You should dress to undress. Like the old saying about wearing nice underwear in case you get hit by a truck. Wear underthings that make you feel good, and you'll look good to others too."

In other words, don't just wear clean underwear in case you need emergency workers, but also in case you need an emergency work-up—by your guy.

Stark wants to remind those of us who need to do something about our moth-eaten undergarments that shopping for lingerie can be a complicated proposition. If you're stumped about what to buy, there are some common choices that will probably work. "A garter belt. Black. Lace. All these things are classic symbols of seduction," she says. "They're also not for everyone. You don't have to assume a different persona. It's really quite simple: just wear something nice." (More lingerie tips to come in Chapter 8.)

Of course, you could always choose to wear nothing at all. "Walking around naked works," says Sasha. "Guys don't always need fancy tactics."

Also, don't leave the flirting to the confines of your house. There's something extremely hot about flirting in public places.

"I took a boyfriend out to meet my friends, and the whole night there was no PDA or anything," says Vicky, a designer in Astoria, New York. "But by the time we were going home in the taxi . . . Oh My God! We were all over each other."

So how do you go from being on your best "I'm a public good girl" behavior to "Oh My God!" in the timespan of a cab ride?

Maren's got some tips. "Caress him under the table when you're out with others," she says. "Give him a great sexy glance when you're at a party."

Sometimes subtlety goes a long way. The people you're with won't necessarily notice. But if you're envisioning the sex position you want to do later while you're flirting with your guy, we're pretty sure he will.

What is Sexy Lingerie?

Sarah Stark, coauthor of The Lingerie Handbook, *recommends looking to the silver screen for inspiration. Here, she shares the most memorable movie moments for intimate apparel:*

It Happened One Night, *1934: "Claudette Colbert borrows Clark Gable's men's pajamas and starts a trend across the country."*

Rear Window, *1954: "Grace Kelly pulls out a frothy pale pink gown with matching satin slippers, showing that femininity has infiltrated the bachelor pad of commitment-phobic James Stewart."*

Baby Doll, *1956: "Carroll Baker sashays around in a short nightgown, a style that eventually gets named after the movie."*

Cat on a Hot Tin Roof, *1958: "Elizabeth Taylor's slip plays a starring role in her attempt to regain the affections of her husband, played by Paul Newman."*

The Graduate, *1967: "Mrs. Robinson's leopard-print slip and bra is all about grown-up seduction for young Benjamin, played by Dustin Hoffman."*

9½ Weeks, *1986: "Kim Basinger wears some sexy things under her power suits. Working women during this time have better jobs and more money, which they often spend on luxurious lingerie."*

Ghost, *1990: "Demi Moore wears her dead husband's T-shirt, part of a trend toward androgynous styles, with women sleeping in oversized tees and boxer shorts."*

The Art of the Arousal

But what if you are like, "Meh" when it comes to sex? You are so over it that you have about as much interest in getting tangled in the sheets ever again as you do in re-chewing an old, worn-out piece of gum. We realize that is why some of you are reading this book. To put it to music, you've lost that lovin' feeling, now it's gone, gone, gone.

You must begin by asking yourself a few questions courtesy of Steinhart: "Are you comfortable with no sex? Are you masturbating at all? Are you thinking about it every once in a while?"

Steinhart suggests, "Maybe you have forgotten to listen to those little twinges or urges, because we forget what to look for sometimes."

Our bodies are complex places. We are reminded repeatedly that sex is bad, and that sex is good. Our bodies are bad, and our bodies are good. Our urges are bad, and our urges are good. No wonder we are so confused! However, most experts will tell you a little nugget that flies in the face of everything you thought about our bodies, ourselves: we have just as much of a propensity to orgasm as men do. In fact, Dr. Kilpatrick insists it isn't our equipment, but how it's used (or misused). "The clitoris," he explains "is a gland located between the labia minora. It has an incredible blood supply and engorges when adequate stimulation is provided and is the source of orgasm in women."

To really drive the point home, when we asked Dr. Altobelli what if any Viagra-type medicine was out there for women, she replied a little indignantly, "*Viagra* is the female Viagra!" Of course our next question was obvious, why is it sold for men? And the good doctor replied, "Because they are rude. Because they think there is a bigger market selling to it men. Because *they* are men! But basically what we have down there is a 'little penis.' When the clitoris engorges it is aroused. Viagra, a vasodilator, helps *dilate* those blood vessels."

That's not to say you should just start popping some dude's Viagra pills. If you really do think you have sexual dysfunction, you should see your doctor for proper treatment. The point is that we have the equipment, and like a man's penis, the clitoris gets bigger and full of blood when it is stimulated. So don't get snowed by the misconception that some women will never be able to come like a man. Our parts are quietly nestled and sometimes require a little unearthing. Men like a challenge, so this should be fun for them. But, perhaps we are the impatient ones.

"We sometimes forget to take a minute and pay attention to what we're feeling," says Steinhart. "Maybe there's a little something. Maybe you're reading a novel and there's a sexy part and you say to yourself, 'There it is again!' Then you should say, out loud this time, 'Honey!'"

Turn It On: Great Tips from the Experts

Change your diet. Experts suggest that eating food high in nutrients and low in fats can have a fantastic effect on your libido. So load up on fruits and veggies and toss the Twinkies.

Learn to be naked. Of course you are born that way. How hard can it be? But experts say it is something that could use a little practice. Try cleaning in the buff when you're home alone. Then get crazy and take it to a nude beach.

Check your labels. Are you taking anything that might be affecting your mojo? If you are on the pill, try a new one. If you are loading up on cough syrup, it often contains alcohol, which can slow you down. Read up on what you are taking and pay attention to your body's reaction to it.

Party more under the sheets, less in the streets. Alcohol and pot are often libido spoilers, so see how much you can cut back on your intake. Remember, your body is a temple.

The Blue Lagoon

We want you to build this oasis, which should include, in addition to calm and comfort, tons of sex. So what happens when you're having trouble getting physically or mentally turned on?

"Ask what it is that is stopping you," suggests Steinhart. "Are you pissed off with him? Maybe there's stuff that's unresolved that you should talk to him about. Maybe you're mad about work."

Or maybe it's that you're starting to forget what's so sexy about your guy. So, notice every time he lifts something and his forearm muscle ripples. Or the way that smile of his really gets you. And then, we want you to go one step even further and *tell him*.

"Don't just look at what's good about your guy, look at what's *sexy*!" suggests Lina.

Also, take inventory of your own behaviors. Say for example, you have a tendency to notice every time your guy chews with his mouth open. Do you also notice the times he doesn't? Going even further, do you often manage to let him know when his open-mouthed chewing is grossing you out? Do you find you are less inclined to tell him how attractive he is on the days he is not? In your day to day, being careful of barraging your guy with negative commentary will ultimately serve both of you.

"Every time my boyfriend does something awesome—even when it's something small like getting the oil changed in my car," says Nina, "I try to show my gratitude. I make a special dinner or take a little extra time 'down there' in the sack."

So, yeah, go ahead and take a minute to think about your favorite things about your guy. Then think of a few ways to reciprocate. Make it a part of your every day, and you will see that you will be on the path to creating your own safe haven between the two of you. But we'd like to take a second to go a step further.

We want to recommend one tried-and-true method if the problem really is coming back to one or both of you just feeling completely apathetic about sex. Sensate focusing is a method developed by sex research pioneers, Masters and Johnson. Simply explained, one person lies on his or her back while the other moves his or her hand over the other's body without coming into contact with the skin. In this way, each partner focuses on his or her own body and its reaction to the warmth of the moving hand. An exercise like this can give both of you an opportunity to tune in to your own body. Other suggestions include rubbing different textures, from cotton to feathers to marble, against each other's skin while blindfolded. Just make sure you do it in the summertime or with the heat cranked; otherwise, it's just plain cold.

Another suggestion, made by multiple sex therapists, is to discuss removing the orgasm as a "goal" with your partner. In so doing, the pressure is taken away. Then the exercise becomes simply about pleasure, without expectation or even culmination.

The fact is, your body is constantly changing from tense to relaxed, comfortable to restless. You will be surprised once you begin looking for its cues, how often you also feel a little something going on between your legs, even when you least expect it.

CHAPTER 6

BIRTH CONTROL AND *OTHER* *SMART* DECISIONS

I'm not really a fan of condoms. Using them doesn't change the way sex feels that much, but it does a little. The problem is that it causes that disconnect when you have to stop and open the package and get the dumb thing on. Plus I always feel a little inept about how to help him put it on. I liked the pill very much when I was on it, but coming off it has messed up my menstrual cycle for almost a year. I'm still not sure if it's back on track yet! So that has been discouraging.

—Amy

HIV Test + The Pill = Commitment?

Before we started writing this book, we didn't know that people had such strong opinions about their birth control. To us, condoms and the pill seem like the most common, effective birth control methods. We figured almost everyone just went ahead and always used one or the other or both. (Unless, of course, they were *trying* to get pregnant.) Seriously, we were really surprised by how many women told us they "sometimes do the wing and a prayer thing," as Randi calls it. Relying on your guy to pull out or on the will of the gods really doesn't work to keep you from getting pregnant, no matter how clever or sincere your prayer. And neither protects you from sexually transmitted diseases (STDs).

The same goes for the "rhythm method"—the practice of abstaining from sex on the most fertile days of your menstrual cycle—which some religious groups teach to married couples not yet ready to conceive. Experts disagree on the effectiveness of this method, but many say it's only about 75 to 85 percent effective, which isn't exactly what we'd call effective. That's like one out of every four times you have sex . . . bam! You're prego.

"The 'pull and pray' method doesn't work," says Melissa L., a chiropractor in Charlottesville, Virginia. "We had a daughter using it, and our friends had twins doing the same!"

Here's the deal with that: Yes, sperm is released while your guy is making his O face. But, sometimes a *leeetle*, tiny bit is released before he ejaculates. All you need is one sperm to fertilize your egg. And, really, do you want to leave your whole future up to your guy's clear, logical thought process in the heat of the moment?

We can't stress this point enough: A condom should be your number-one birth control choice. And you should use it every time you have sex. We're serious. So serious. We're like Peyton Manning's game face right before the Super Bowl. We're like the feeling in the room right after your boss overheard your cube-mate talking smack about her. We're like the case of food poisoning you got when you tried those clams at the shady oceanside food truck. In fact, we're way more serious than any of those things.

Other than abstinence, condoms are the only way to effectively prevent STDs. According to Avert.org, an organization committed to fighting AIDS worldwide, the instance of chlamydia cases doubled from half a million cases in 1996 to over a million in 2006. Chlamydia is a bacterial infection sometimes known as the "silent epidemic" because as many as 75 percent of cases in women are completely symptom-free. It is the most common STD found in humans. Ranking second is gonorrhea, with nearly 400,000 new cases appearing in the United States in 2006. Gonorrhea, like chlamydia, is often hard to detect in both men and women, and if left untreated, could severely compromise your reproductive system. While both chlamydia and gonorrhea can be cured with treatment, both are also preventable by using condoms.

A 2008 study revealed that 26 percent of American women between fourteen and nineteen are already infected with one of the four most-common STDs, including HPV (human papillomavirus, an incurable virus which can lead to genital warts or in some cases, cervical cancer), chlamydia, herpes simplex virus (also incurable, this virus leads to painful open sores), and trichomoniasis (an uncomfortable parasite that can cause extreme itching and burning where you don't watch to itch or burn). For more info on a whole range of possible fun-between-the-legs STDs, check out the Centers for Disease Control at *www.cdc.gov*.

Now, let us repeat, with emphasis, what we've just said: *one in four* women has a serious STD before the age of twenty! We'd also like to mention that the latest surveillance data for 2007 is saying that the number of AIDS cases has ballooned by 15 percent since 2004 in a sampling of thirty-four states—this is not an epidemic that ended with the '80s. Think about that before your guy gives you his sweetest puppy-dog eyes and reminds you how much better it feels without a condom. Before you make an educated choice as a couple to take off the condom, get everyone a checkup and talk to each other about what's going on in people's pants out there as a reminder that if anyone strays, there is real danger, and we're not just talking about the threat of key scratches on his Land Rover or heartbreak.

"I have seen a half dozen cases of syphilis within the last couple months," says Dr. Kilpatrick. And, dude, syphilis is frickin' scary. We're talking, damage-to-all-major-organs-if-left-untreated scary.

Remember that even if your guy is wonderful, loving, sweet, and hygienic, he could have something he could pass along to you. In fact, he might not even know it. You might have something you don't know about either. Depending on the disease, some people can be "carriers." They feel perfectly normal but can infect other people. Remind your guy that even those STDs that hardly affect men at all can sometimes lead to infertility, severe pain, or, in extreme cases, death. If he still doesn't get it, ask him what he'd want his sister or daughter to do if she were in your position. We think this will help him get his head back in his brain and out of his crotch.

Oh, we know what you're thinking: "Thanks for the lecture, guys. We took Sex Ed too, and we get it. But at this point we both know we're disease-free, we trust each other, and even though we're not ready for baby making, we are sick and tired of condoms and know there are alternative birth-control options out there. We want to explore them. Step away from your soap box and tell us what they are already!"

Okay, okay. Maybe you're right. Renee thinks so: "If you're in a long-term relationship, and you take certain tests to find out that you're both healthy, I personally think that not using condoms and using the pill is okay."

But proceed with caution, says Valerie: "I'd say use the condom until you are 100 percent sure you are going to marry this guy," she says. "Even after you are married, you never *really* know, so I think it's best to be safe than sorry."

The key here is trust. You have to know in your heart—and your head—that your guy isn't going to be cheating on you. Ever.

It's kind of like when Elaine on *Seinfeld* only had a limited supply of sponges and started interviewing her boyfriend to see if he was "sponge-worthy." Is this guy utterly and completely worth giving up the protection and peace of mind that only condoms offer?

And, as much as you trust him, we recommend being extra cautious about trusting him to get his STD testing done well and done thoroughly.

Maybe you could make it a ceremonious thing. Make your calls to your respective doctors together (you're in this together to support each other!). Then you each make your visits, asking for every STD test known to man. Then, a couple of weeks later you meet up somewhere and exchange results. Hell, physically exchange papers. See the clean bills of health for yourselves, then cross arms and drink from each other's glasses of celebratory champagne. If, on the other hand, those bills of health are not so healthy, then decide together how to proceed. And thank yourself for having been so ridiculously smart to have had this done. Also, remember to be honest and respectful. Having an STD doesn't make anyone a bad person. Just knowing the statistics out there, it's probably fair to say it could happen to anyone. It should just make you both act extra carefully in the future.

We Asked. He Answered.

Q: *How can a woman get her guy to wear a condom when he doesn't want to?*

A: Best way, I would think, is for her to learn how to put it on him with her mouth. —DAVID

The Battle Between Pills and Rubbers—Who Will Reign Supreme?

Ah, so as we mentioned, pills and condoms are pretty popular as far as birth control goes. Most women we spoke to didn't know much about the other options out there. Case in point? Sasha: "I haven't tried anything other than condoms and the pill," she says. And that's perfectly well and good, as long as they're working for you.

But we also found that these two forms of birth control have created some love-hate relationships with their users.

For example, Courtney sings the praises of condoms. "Without them, it's really messy," she says. But Holly's not so keen. "Condoms smell and interrupt the moment," she says.

Sharon is a fan of the birth control pill. "It regulates my period, helps reduce my endometriosis pain, prevents pregnancy—and the kind I'm on allows me to only have four periods per year," she says.

Some other ladies? Not so much.

"I can't do the pill because it screws up my singing," says Leah, an opera singer in Knoxville, Tennessee. "And that's nonnegotiable. It's my job."

"I don't like taking all those hormones," says Randi.

"I had a hard time remembering to take the pill every day at the same time," says Tara.

"I swear that the pill totally messed with my libido," says Karen, a publicist in Los Angeles. "I was about as sexual as a beanbag while I was on it."

"I was on the wrong pill for a while and really started to think I just didn't care about sex!" says Simona. "Then one day I was like, hmm, I've never not cared about sex before. So, I switched brands. Turns out, I care about sex."

This is a common complaint, which some studies have validated and others haven't quite been able to prove. But, if you feel that your pill is thwarting your urge to get down and dirty, Dr. Kilpatrick says you're not imagining it. "[Oral contraceptive] use *can* decrease a woman's desire," he says. In this case, we think it's worth looking into other brands—or other methods all together (Check out our "Birth

Control Refresher Course" for ideas.). With all these strong opinions, there's also the potential for disagreement with your guy. So, what do you do if you're an "I hate the pill" girl, and he's an "I can't stand condoms" guy?

Well, we think you've got a leg up on him with this argument (pun intended). What we mean is that the "pros" of condom use are much stronger: no STDs and no hormones (which sometimes put your health at risk). Plus, there's always the "no glove, no love" ultimatum. We think if he's given the option of wearing a condom or not getting any, he's sure as hell wearing a condom. (For more on this, read on to the section "Helping Condoms to Take Back the Power.")

But, if you really want a compromise, Steinhart recommends trying the female condom. "They're a riot," she says. "They're like baggies. People hate them because they're weird initially of course, and because they're noisy. You need two things if you're gonna use them. You need a sense of humor, and you need extra lube. The more lube there is, the less sound there is. They're ridiculous, but why not! Give yourself another option."

And, if you've done STD testing, talk to your doctor about your other birth control options. If you're looking for ideas, we've outlined a bunch for you. It is only a sampling, so if your interest has been piqued, we strongly suggest you look into some other ideas yourself. We think you'll be surprised to discover that even Mr. Sweaty-gross-sex-ed-teacher missed a lot of these.

A Birth Control Refresher Course

We know it's been a while since health class, so maybe you're wondering exactly what your options are. There have been some major technological advancements since the tenth grade. Those are listed here, along with some old faithfuls. Of course, always check with your doctor for the entire scoop, but hopefully these will give you some food for thought:

The Method: Condom

What It Is: *By now you know what a rubber is. If you don't, use Google, damn it.*

Why It Might Be Right for You: *You're an intelligent women looking to protect herself from pregnancy and STDs. Remember that even if you're using other birth control methods, it's always a good idea to use condoms, too.*

Potential Risks: *Irritation and allergic reactions (Allergic to latex? Try the polyurethane kind.)*

Effectiveness Against Pregnancy: *About 84 to 89 percent*

How to Get It: *Over the counter at your local pharmacy or supermarket. We like when they're handed out for free at concerts and stuff, but the ones you see in jars at bars or clubs can be suspect. Like it or not, condoms (like an undervalued sex life) don't age well.*

Our Two Cents: *As we mentioned before, the condom is the hands-down best way for sexually active people to prevent the spread of STDs, and it's pretty darn effective with pregnancy too. Try a few different brands to see which feels best to you. And, like we said, double-check expiration dates.*

The Method: Female Condom

What It Is: *Picture a regular condom all unfurled and flappy with a flexible ring on the closed end that you insert into your lady parts.*

Why It Might Be Right for You: *You're not liking how the typical condom feels during sex, but you still want to protect against STDs.*

Potential Risks: *Allergic reaction and irritation*
Effectiveness Against Pregnancy: *About 80 percent*
How to Get It: *Over the counter*
Our Two Cents: *The female condom isn't as effective against pregnancy as the typical condom. It's also not as effective against STDs. And remember what Steinhart said about the funny sound it makes.*

The Method: Diaphragm

What It Is: *A curved disk you cover with spermicide and insert into your vagina before you have sex so it covers your cervix. It must be kept in for at least six hours afterward.*

Why It Might Be Right for You: *You don't mind sticking stuff up there, and you're really good at saying, "Okay, hold that thought. I need five minutes in the bathroom before we go any further." Alternatively, some people like this method of birth control because you can wear it comfortably for twenty-four hours before it needs a good cleaning. This means you don't necessarily have to "break" before sex if you know earlier in the evening that the good stuff is coming. But reapply the spermicide if you are on round two — or three or more.*

Potential Risks: *Irritation, allergic reactions, urinary tract infections (UTIs), toxic shock syndrome (you know, the tampon disease)*
Effectiveness Against Pregnancy: *About 85 percent*
How to Get It: *You must get fitted by a doctor.*
Our Two Cents: *Aside from the complicated insertion stuff, when used correctly and cleaned often, diaphragms are a safe and fairly effective way to avoid any unwanted deliveries from the stork. Plus, it allows you to have condom-free sex without the hormones.*

The Method: Cervical Cap

What It Is: *It's a round rubber cup with a rim that fits around your cervix.*

Why It Might Be Right for You: *Similar to the diaphragm, a cervical cap can be left in for forty-eight hours (while the diaphragm must go after twenty-four), and if you have sex for a second (or third or fourth) time during that period, you don't have to reapply spermicide to it.*

Potential Risks: *Irritation, allergic reactions, abnormal Pap smear results, toxic shock*

Effectiveness Against Pregnancy: *About 77 to 83 percent*

How to Get It: *From your doctor*

Our Two Cents: *It can be difficult to insert properly, which we're pretty sure accounts for the discrepancy in effectiveness. Therefore, we like the odds for the diaphragm better.*

The Method: Spermicide

What It Is: *Spermicide comes in many forms, from foams to creams to jellies; you can also find it in film form, as a suppository, or a tablet. Spermicide contains nonoxynol-9, a chemical that kills sperm. You insert it into your nether regions (also known as "up your cooch") five to ninety minutes before sex.*

Why It Might Be Right for You: *If the diaphragm and cervical caps are too tricked out for your limited dexterity and you already know that condoms and the pill are wrong for you, this method is simple and effective. Because it is a liquid, once it goes in, it will spread out to all your nooks and crannies, thereby doing the hard work for you, including keeping you from getting an unwanted plus sign in a bathroom stall four weeks later.*

Potential Risks: *Irritation, allergic reactions, UTIs*

Effectiveness Against Pregnancy: *About 70 percent*

How to Get It: *Over the counter*

Our Two Cents: *Seventy percent isn't really good enough for us. It's a fantastic idea to use spermicides in conjunction with other methods. (Just be sure the kind you use is compatible with condoms—you don't want to choose something that can break down rubber.) If you do use them, make sure you clean yourself up thoroughly afterward—as you should after any sex—to avoid UTIs and yeast infections.*

The Method: Combined (Estrogen and Progestin) Pill

What It Is: *These are typical oral contraceptives. You take one by mouth at about the same time every day. The combination of hormones tricks your body into thinking you're pregnant, so you don't ovulate. Usually there's a "placebo" week of pills (usually made of nothing more exciting than sugar) during which you get your period.*

Why It Might Be Right for You: *The pill is a good option if you're in a committed relationship, both of you are free of STDs, and you don't smoke. Also, make sure you're good at remembering to take it everyday and don't mind refilling a prescription every month.*

Potential Risks: *Dizziness, nausea, changes in your menstrual cycle, changes in mood, weight gain, high blood pressure, blood clots, heart attack, stroke*

Effectiveness Against Pregnancy: *About 95 percent*

How to Get It: *By prescription*

Our Two Cents: *Beware of health risks and pay attention to how your body reacts to this pill—everyone's different. Work closely with your gynecologist to find the right pill, and in addition to no babies, you could also have great skin, decreased appetite, and way less cramping and PMS-related moodiness. Some can even make your period lighter! The* *new extended and continuous-use pills, which allow you to have less frequent periods—or none at all—are said to be just as safe and effective at preventing pregnancy. But again, we insist you go over everything with your doctor. Also, if you smoke, be extra careful.*

The Method: Progestin-only Pill

What It Is: *This is like the combined pill, only it's just progestin. This hormone prevents sperm from getting to the egg by thickening cervical mucus. Gross, we know. (We said "mucus.") Don't worry. It doesn't leak or anything.*

Why It Might Be Right for You: *You like the idea of a birth control pill, but you smoke or have certain health concerns. This pill has less cardiovascular risks than the combined pill. Some studies have said that it's slightly less effective in preventing pregnancy than the combined pill.*

Potential Risks: *Irregular bleeding, weight gain, breast tenderness*

Effectiveness Against Pregnancy: *About 95 percent*

How to Get It: *By prescription*

Our Two Cents: *See our thoughts on the "combined pill"; they are about the same, minus the smoking thing.*

The Method: Injections (Depo-Provera and Lunelle)

What It Is: *These are shots your doctor can give you once every three months. They include the same hormones as birth control pills.*

Why It Might Be Right for You: *You're not good at remembering to take a pill every day, but you're good at keeping appointments every few months.*

Potential Risks: *Bone loss, bleeding between periods, weight gain, breast tenderness, headaches*

Effectiveness Against Pregnancy: *About 99 percent*

How to Get It: *During doctor's visits every three months*

Our Two Cents: *There's less room for human error here or at least, non-medically trained human error, so it's pretty darn effective. We think that little pinprick of pain is probably worth it. But check with your health insurance—that's four annual doctor's appointments you need to make sure you can afford!*

The Method: NuvaRing

What It Is: *Maybe you've seen the commercials with the woman's hand squeezing this soft ring. You insert it into your vagina, keep it in for three weeks, then remove it for a week. Then start the routine over again. It, too, works with hormones.*

Why It Might Be Right For You: *Again with the not remembering to take something every day. Or maybe taking pills by mouth upsets your stomach.*

Potential Risks: *Vaginal discharge, swelling of the vagina, irritation, and the risks associated with oral contraceptives*

Effectiveness Against Pregnancy: *About 95 percent*

How to Get It: *By prescription*

Our Two Cents: *Maybe it's just us, but we think it might be harder to remember to keep up this routine than it is to take something once a day. Maybe marking it on your calendar or setting an alarm on your cell phone could help.*

The Method: Emergency Contraceptives (Preven or Plan B)

What It Is: *The infamous "morning-after pill," this contains hormones that help prevent the sperm that have already entered your body from fertilizing your egg. It won't, however, end an existing pregnancy. (There is an "abortion pill," but that is a whole different banana.)*

Why It Might Be Right for You: *Your condom broke—or you made a major error in judgment within the last seventy-two hours. (Or sometimes in cases of sexual assault.) The sooner you use it, the better your chances of preventing pregnancy.*

Potential Risks: *Nausea, ectopic pregnancy (in the event that it fails to prevent pregnancy), irregular bleeding, breast tenderness, fatigue, headache, abdominal pain, and dizziness, all of which should subside after you are done taking it (Luckily you only take two doses.)*

Effectiveness Against Pregnancy: *About 85 percent*

How to Get It: *By prescription (Plan B is now available over the counter at pharmacies for women over age seventeen.)*

Our Two Cents: *The morning-after pill is a great way to prevent pregnancy in the event of an accident, lapse in judgment, or sudden panic that you are not ready to be a mom. However, due to the high hormone dosage administered and the general cost-effectiveness, using the morning-after pill as a regular form of birth control is not the way to go.*

The Method: IUD (ParaGard or Mirena)

What It Is: *Intrauterine Device. You guessed it—it goes in your uterus and prevents pregnancy with the same hormones as birth control pills and the like. A doctor inserts this T-shaped doo-hickey for you, and it can stay in place from one to ten years, depending on the brand.*

Why It Might Be Right for You: *You really can't remember to take pills, and you know you don't want to have babies for at least one year—that's how long you usually have to wait once it has been removed before trying to get pregnant.*

Potential Risks: *Cramps, bleeding, pelvic inflammatory disease, infertility, and perforation of uterus. Women with certain health conditions should be wary.*

Effectiveness Against Pregnancy: *About 99 percent*

How to Get It: *By prescription*

Our Two Cents: *Try it if you're healthy and aren't creeped out knowing there's a foreign object (which supposedly you can't feel) hanging out up there.*

The Method: The Rhythm Method

What It Is: *Abstaining from sex during a woman's most fertile days. It requires you to closely monitor your body—checking your temperature and the viscosity of your vaginal discharge (yup, we said it) are part of the deal.*

Why It Might Be Right for You: *You're married or long-term cohabiting, and while you're not* trying *per se to have kids, it wouldn't be the end of the world if you did. Also, the idea of vaginal discharge and checking its "viscosity" doesn't gross you out.*

Potential Risks: *None, except pregnancy. No matter how diligent you are, you are an imperfect human being with a body with cycles that aren't completely predictable. Sorry, but examining the contents of your underpants isn't an exact science.*

Effectiveness Against Pregnancy: *About 75 to 85 percent*

How to Get It: *Ask your doctor for information and stick to the plan.*

Our Two Cents: *We think you're going to be really, really horny on the days you're supposed to be abstaining. Also, remember that sperm can live in the body for days on end, and your ovulation isn't set to the official World Clock, so you're really pushing your luck here. But we hear you that seeing the lists of health risks all over this chart (including words like "irritation," "stroke," and that thing about the opera singer's voice changing) is enough to make anyone ready to break out the thermometer,* *get out the colored pencils, and burn some incense in the hopes that they can thwart pregnancy in some organic way.*

The Method: Sterilization

What It Is: *A surgery that permanently ends your—or his— ability to conceive. For women, there are several options that block the fallopian tubes, which is where the sperm and egg usually meet. Your guy could be sterilized too. His vas deferens would be cut, preventing sperm from traveling from the testicles to the penis.*

Why It Might Be Right for You: *You already have kids and are 100 percent certain you don't want to add to your family. And will never change your mind. Ever.*

Potential Risks: *Pain, bleeding infection, ectopic pregnancy (for women), plus the usual risks associated with surgery. Risk factors highly depend on the method of sterilization you choose.*

Effectiveness Against Pregnancy: *About 99 percent*

How to Get It: *Surgery*

Our Two Cents: *We don't encourage making permanent changes to your body—we don't even want you to get a tattoo—but if pregnancy could jeopardize your health or is completely out of the equation for you, go ahead and talk to your doctor. Oh yeah, and the guy version (vasectomy) is supposedly less invasive than the options for women.*

The Method: The Sponge

What It Is: *A soft, round, foam sponge about 2 inches in diameter that you insert deep into your vagina before intercourse. It is made of plastic foam and contains spermicide. A nylon loop at the bottom helps with removal when you are done with sex.*

Why It Might Be Right for You: *Again, you don't mind sticking stuff up there, and you like the idea of being protected in two ways: (1) because it blocks the cervix to keep sperm from entering and (2) it releases spermicide to stop the ones that slip by.*

Potential Risks: *It can cause problems if you are allergic to sulfa drugs or the things that make up the sponge—polyurethane and spermicide. Do not use it if you have recently had an abortion, given birth, or miscarried. Also, using it while on your period can increase your chances for toxic shock syndrome.*

Effectiveness Against Pregnancy: *About 75 percent*

How to Get It: *Since they are only recently back on the market after a hiatus, the easiest way to get them is online, however some family planning centers and drugstores are beginning to carry them again for $9 to $15 for a pack of three.*

Our Two Cents: *The sponge can be difficult to correctly insert. Women who have had children have a higher chance of accidental pregnancy while using the sponge. However, it is an easy alternative to condoms and provides more protection than spermicide alone. Just make sure you can stay committed to using them.*

Prescription Birth Control Picks and Pans

What are other women using, and how do they like them?

"I took Seasonale. That's the pill where you get your period four times a year. When I was on it, it was fine, but then when I came off of it my cycle was crazy and my skin broke out." —AMY

"I'm using a new pill, Lybrel. It has no placebos, so you don't get your period, at all. I loved it at first, but then I started to have spotting and discovered that about 70 percent of women who take it have spotting. That's a big percent! Plus, I can see where those who are paranoid about pregnancy might need to have their period to stay sane." —SASHA

"Several of my friends had problems with IUDs, like ectopic pregnancies and infections." —MAREN

"I have been on the same pill for fifteen years. It is Ortho Novum, and it's great for me, because I have had no side effects, and it regulates my periods." —RACHEL

"I used the patch in the past, which I loved, but then they started warning women about the increased chance of blood clots—even more so than with the pill—and my doctor suggested I go off it. If they ever create a patch that doesn't have that health risk, I'll go back on it in a second. That sucker never fell off—even during water-skiing—and I loved not having to take the pill every day." —ALEXANDRA

"With my old birth control pill, I was getting migraines right before every period. When I told my doctor, she put me on Mircette. It definitely helped me have less headaches, but didn't get rid of them completely." —TARA

What's Up, Doc?

While you should have a conversation with your own doctor if you're interested in the pill, for a little extra insight, we posed some tough questions about birth control to Dr. Charles Kilpatrick.

Q: There are some new forms of birth control, like the Nuva Ring and the Lunelle shot. Are they better or worse than older ones?

A: Neither. [Hormonal] birth control options have the same effective ingredients. They're just packaged differently—as pills, injections, IUDs, or implants. The dose of hormones they deliver may vary, however.

Q: We heard that women who smoke or are over age thirty-five shouldn't take the pill. What other options do you recommend for these women?

A: Birth control pills that have a combination of progesterone and estrogen can increase the likelihood of blood clotting in a woman's body. This is extra risky for smokers and women with liver disease. There is no specific [proven] age cut-off though. A woman at risk could try a progesterone-only birth control method, which can come in the form of an IUD, an implant or pills. If she's through with childbearing, permanent sterilization is effective as well.

Q: Many women worry about staying on the pill for years and years at a time. Is this risky?

A: Extended use of the pill is fine. The combined oral contraceptive pill (estrogen and progesterone) is safe to take until menopause, granted you are not a heavy smoker (more than fifteen cigarettes a day) or have underlying hypertension. (The estrogen component in the oral contraceptive pill can increase clotting factors and slightly elevate blood pressure, so I put some women with very well controlled blood pressure on it, but not if they have other underlying problems from their high blood pressure.)

When you get to menopause there are lower doses [of the pill] for hormone replacement that you can take if you have symptoms, although I know some women who still take them in their fifties. [However, it is] not well studied, and it seems that women are beginning to catch up to men as far as coronary artery disease, heart disease, etc., go, so we no longer recommend hormones like we used to.

Helping Condoms to Take Back the Power

Ah, you thought we were done. You thought, "Finally, they are going to give it a rest." There you were, setting up your appointment to talk to your doctor about the cervical cap when all of the sudden we are back, with more talk of the condom. We understand that this is a book about keeping long-term relationships hot. And "long-term relationship" means you are all trusting and in love. It means that you are his hot tamale, and he is your big manly bear. You guys don't need us to tell you that you have to use condoms, not now, not when you're barely getting any. At least not enough worth writing home about . . .

Okay, but here's the thing. We'd be doing you a dis-service if we didn't talk to you about condoms in a different way than you've ever heard before, like a sit-you-down, hold-your-hand talk to you about them, especially if you fit one of the following scenarios (you only have to answer to yourself so don't lie, because you hate it when you lie . . .):

1. You or your guy is a cheater.
2. You are wondering if his lack of interest in your sex life might possibly, even in an alternate universe, have to do with your guy being a cheater.
3. You have been together for a while, but neither of you has been tested for STDs in the past six months to a year.
4. You are relatively new to this relationship, and it's hard to tell when he's lying at this point.

We don't want to imply that you should become really insecure or paranoid. But the thing is, this is your life you are playing with. Just look at the news! Unwanted pregnancies are on the rise, and STDs are reaching epidemic proportions. So, we are writing this section whether you want to read it or not. But we really want you to read it. That's how important we think this is.

We've already gone over what needs to happen before you decide to go off the condom, but what should you do to convince yourself and your man that staying on it is the right thing for the time being?

"There are some really cool condoms out there that are just interesting," says Nina.

In fact, why not tell your boyfriend you think it would be fun to try out every weird, crazy condom out there, just to give it a whirl? (Some, in fact, do whirl.) We bet if you mention the flavored ones, he'll get on board.

Or don't ask, just provide. "You should have condoms with you too. It isn't just the guy's responsibility," says Vicky. Just presenting a condom at the critical point makes not using it less likely than both partners shrugging and saying, "I don't have one on me . . ."

Steinhart wants you to remind your guy that protecting *yourself* makes condoms important. "It's tough," she concedes. "But do you want to be with someone who won't protect himself or you?"

When we discussed using condoms with Steinhart, she asked us what excuses guys were likely to give for not using condoms. We answered that they would say it didn't feel as good. She told us, "You're absolutely right. Neither does getting sick."

The truth is, condom-free sex might feel better than condom-full sex, but the alternative, say, herpes, is going to feel a whole lot worse than sex with a condom ever could.

"It's like saying heroine feels better than pot," says Eleanor. "It may be true but you still shouldn't make a lifestyle out of it."

You might even try to convince your guy that you actually *like* how condoms feel. "I never got it when people say the condoms don't feel good," says Tara. "Maybe I'm the only one, but there's something about the way the tip touches me during sex; it's an excellent sensation."

Now, let's say for a minute that you are one of those one in four women with an STD. With a statistic like 23 percent of women and 11 percent of men in their 20s carrying the herpes virus, there is a decent chance that you are. Perhaps some of the problems you and your guy are facing in the bedroom is a direct result of your own insecurities or even perhaps a sense of betrayal, anger, or embarrassment at having been infected with an STD in the first place.

"When I found out I had HPV I felt so dirty," says Courtney. "But life goes on."

If you don't have the same attitude as Courtney, maybe you need to seek the help of a professional. A therapist can help you with some of your negative feelings toward sex.

However, one way to take back the power your STD has over your life is to commit to condoms. Learn to enjoy them. They are the best way to keep you and your partner safe. And follow the advice of your doctor to stay healthy even if you have an incurable virus like HIV, herpes, or HPV. There are ways to live a full and healthy life, with sex!

Until the day you and your partner are clear with each other about the risks unprotected sex pose to each of you and vow to keep each other safe no matter what, it is your responsibility to your body to keep those rubbers on!

The World of Condoms

Go to Condom Country online (*www.condom.com*) to find any of the following zany developments in condom technology:

- *Trojan Her Pleasure with Warm Sensations*: This space-age condom claims to release "gentle waves of pleasure at the most intimate of moments."
- *Beyond Seven Studded Condom*: We aren't totally sure what they mean by "studded," but we feel safe assuming the studs are bumps in the latex, and not, like, metal and pointy. Ouch.
- *Trustex Flavored Condoms*: Chocolate, Strawberry, Banana, Vanilla, Grape, Cola, and Mint. Mmm.

- *Night Light Glow in the Dark Condoms*: This condom glows in the dark for thirty seconds. We guess that it's so that he can find the correct place to insert his business, which you will find helpful in the middle of your fit of hysterical laughter.
- *Santa Condom Pops*: It bears the likeness of Father Christmas on the outside and carries the *spirit* of Christmas inside.
- *Kling-Tite Naturalamb*: This natural-membrane condom (made from lamb skin) will prevent pregnancy, but not STDs. So, make sure, if you are concerned about STDs, you stick to latex or polyurethane.

Saying No

We are spending a lot of time in this book letting you know that it's okay to say to yes to sex sometimes, even when you aren't sure you want it. However, giving yourself permission to say no can in fact help your relationship too. In other words, set some standards. If your guy won't get tested for STDs and doesn't want to use a condom, tell him that there will be no sex. Similarly if your guy isn't trying to help you get turned on, if he's one of those pushing-your-head-toward-his-business people, you have our permission to put on the breaks. Tell him that you require more than a head push to get turned on. Be specific. Often, when your guy sees that you are taking control of your body, he will respect you for it. And he certainly will if he cares at all about you and your well-being, mental and physical. If you feel that using a condom will ease some of your mental anxieties about sex, for example, that is a sound and reasonable argument. Help him to understand where you are coming from.

We Asked. He Answered.

Q: When is it okay for a woman to say no to sex with a long-term partner?

A: *When she's not horny. When she doesn't want it. When she's sick. If you've been a colossal dick. But when it's been longer than a week, the pressure builds up and it starts getting awkward and weird. Trust me, I was fucking married, and I can count how many times I had sex in calendar year 1997 on two hands. That shit ain't right. —HENRY*

"Sometimes letting him know that it isn't forever can help him to see it your way," suggests Vanessa. "Like, you're working through something. You need his help."

Guys like to be needed. And it's okay to be vulnerable about things related to your sexuality. Intimacy can be scary. A good person should be willing to help you move forward.

Want to say no because you're not in the mood? "Sometimes if you're distracted, you need to be able to say, 'I'm sorry. Maybe we can try again in an hour,'" says Steinhart. "Sometimes that distraction is present and it's smart to pay attention to."

Or maybe it's not. Maybe you can *get* in the mood if you just let go of whatever else is going on and concentrate on getting it on. "Telling him you need a little foreplay beforehand sometimes helps," says Eleanor.

Ask for what you want. Some kissing, some fondling. And then make it clear, if you still don't want it, no one's getting it.

"It's always okay to say no to my boyfriend," says Alexandra. "Sex is only good when we're both into it and he cares enough about me to realize that when I'm not in the mood, there's a reason, like I'm not feeling good—physically or emotionally."

Allowing yourself to say no when your body isn't physically responding is a good way to take off some of the mental pressure. We ladies are quite heady when it comes to sex. Somehow, just letting ourselves off the hook is enough to help us enjoy sex even more.

Laura agrees, "Whenever your heart and mind are not into it, say no. It is better to say no, than to fake it."

Sharon feels very strongly about this issue. When we asked her when it was okay to turn your partner down she replied with authority, "*Whenever!*"

Set the bar so that sex only happens between two comfortable and aroused individuals. We think that's an excellent plan as long as you dedicate some time to working with your man to figure out the comfort and the arousal part.

CHAPTER 7

IDENTIFYING PROBLEMS— AND SOLVING THEM *FOR GOOD*

> In the beginning the dog and I were both so excited when he got home from work. She'd pee on herself, and I'd cover him in kisses. Now he's lucky if he gets so much of a tail wag from either of us.

—Vanessa

Spicing It Up

We'd quote the Spice Girls about what you really, really want here, but we're not allowed for copyright reasons.

Even though telling your guy what you want is often the least easy proposition in the world, it's remarkable how much simpler *getting* it becomes the minute you can name exactly what it is. Let's start with a simple assumption: You want something different than what you already have. When we begin changing things in our lives, it's important to consider what we want those changes to be. If you want to meet goals that will ultimately help you achieve a new level of intimacy, sexiness, and mad lovin' under the sheets, well, we think we can help you out with that.

Don't you wish there was some specific path to great long-term sex with your love? Like, "Turn left at the fire hydrant, grab the pack of magic condoms, put one on and . . . whoosh!" We'd like to say that a simple acknowledgment of a goal, any goal, is one great way to if not trail-blaze a direct line to fantasmarific sex, at least begin to see a few palm trees in the distance that indicate an oasis is near. And where there is an oasis there is blue water. And in that blue water you are naked and playfully splashing your man. It's a metaphor for awesome sex. Get it? Well, you will soon, we hope!

You have decided that you want a spicier sex life. We have already gone over ways to sexify your bedroom, ways to keep the riff-raff out of Club Sexy, and suggestions for making more time for sex. Now we want to arm you with a plan that is almost guaranteed to drop you off at the door of a great sex life.

What exactly is missing in your relationship? In our assessment there are a few key problems that might lead a gal to a book like this: (1) you just don't want it like you used to; (2) he is more interested in World of Warcraft than your sweet ass; or (3) you are both more interested in your careers/chores/kids/stressors than in anything naked and writhing. Of course, it may be a combination of all three. What matters is not pointing fingers or placing blame, but rather, knowing that both of you are responsible for the future of your relationship. You can improve your sex life together. So, whatever your unique problem may be, it can be solved. And we're here to provide ideas that will help you do just that. Keep reading for them.

It's Not You; It's Me

So say you haven't been feeling too randy lately, and you're wondering how to get back on the sexual wagon. Listen, honey, you have all the power—like you've been wearing the ruby slippers all along and with just a few clicks . . . ! Okay, not quite that easy—but think about it. You don't have to talk anyone into anything other than yourself.

We know you've picked up this book, so obviously you believe that sex is an important part of your relationship. Or someone does. Like your man. But do *you*? Do you really? Sometimes you are just thinking things like, "But it's fine! I mean if he said we never had to do it again, I'd be totally okay with that."

First of all, we'd like to encourage you to remember all those wonderful amazing things that sex brings to your relationship! And let's face it, aren't we all in a better mood and easier to be around when we're getting laid? If you or your partner is unhappy with the frequency and quality of sex in your relationship, it can add another point of contention to a relationship that really should be a comfortable situation for you both. Having a *friendship* with your guy is great—but your relationship should be everything both of you want it to be. And if you want to be your man's friend, lover, and everything in between, this is most certainly possible.

First, identify where it all began to go wrong. "I put on a few pounds and just haven't felt sexy since," says Marcie, a financial planner in Dearborn, Michigan. If you are having trouble seeing yourself as sexual, maybe you have also had a change in your body image or self-perception.

Insecurities happen. We'd like to remind you of the self you were when you were ten pounds lighter—were you walking around cursing your elephant thighs then too? Probably. So accept your ten pounds *heavier* self, and start loving your body now! The truth is, breaking yourself out of the negative body-image cycle is a whole other book. But since you're reading this one, we'd like to ask that you stop pointing and laughing at yourself. Give yourself a break. Instead of focusing on the moments your man would rather watch the game than caress your silky skin, pay attention to all those times he can't keep his mitts off you. Allow yourself to feel wanted and to believe in the wanting.

And we really must insist: Do not, under any circumstances, stand in front of a full-length mirror, whining, asking your guy, "Do these jeans make me look fat?" Guys hear these seven words and panic. They think they're being cornered, that no matter what they say, they're going to say the wrong thing, and they, inevitably, wind up *saying the wrong thing.* Bringing him into your insecurities and making him a part of them is a rookie mistake we've all made. But the first thing to acknowledge is that, more often than not, he barely noticed the ten inches you had cut off your long blond hair last month, much less the effect that the pizza slice you had for lunch has had on your saddle bags. Instead, ask *yourself*, "Do these jeans make me look fat?" And answer, "No. They make me look beautiful." In other words, get the right answer the first time. And, hell, if you really think they do, step out of them, burn them, and find a pair that's flattering.

Getting off the negative body-image train can be a tough prospect, what with it going 100 miles over steep mountains and you carrying all that baggage. But there are a few things that can be done to help you feel better about yourself. You could try setting up a girl's trip with your most supportive friends to buy some new clothes that fit better than the old ones. Get a push-up bra that accents your increased cleavage. A spa day is a great way to do something loving for yourself. A facial might help calm winter skin or tame an oily summer complexion. Even if you aren't a hippie, giving yourself daily affirmations that yes, you are beautiful and sexy, no matter what's changed in your life, can be deeply beneficial. All you have to do is believe yourself.

If your guy tends to be negative about your body, it might be a good idea to tell him that you are worried that it is affecting how you feel about yourself. If, on the other hand, your guy's been telling you how hot you are, this problem might be all you. Try going to the gym. We're not saying you necessarily need to lose weight. We're saying that exercise helps build self-confidence and a positive attitude. We also think you'll be more energetic in the sack. Remember when Dr. Kilpatrick said that being in good shape should make sex better for you? Well, he did.

Dr. Altobelli reiterates, "When you sweat, pheromones are released. I'm not saying to forget showering, but sometimes a little sweat can actually help your cause."

Napoleon once wrote to his beloved Josephine: "I will return soon from war. Do not wash so that I may enjoy all of your natural aromas."

The trick here is defining goals. If you are serious about meeting your and your man's sexual needs, figure out how to become authentically attracted to him again. Perhaps you see him more as a couch warmer these days and less like the hot stud he was when you first met. You can't force anyone to go to the gym or to stop slurping his spaghetti. What you can do is change how you are seeing and treating him.

Pay attention to the language you're using when you speak to him. Are you lecturing him about his incessant Xbox playing, or his inexplicable inability to identify a burnt-out light bulb and replace it? Not only could these words and thoughts be taking a toll on his self-esteem, but they could be hurting your own opinion of him. Tread lightly here!

Take him out of his context. Go away for a few days, take a dance class together, and find ways to reintroduce yourselves.

"My guy and I started meeting up for lunches during the workday," says Tara. "There's something really sexy about seeing each other away from the house and all the chores and bills and to-do lists. It's almost like we're having a secret tryst. It's exciting."

Also, remember not to take sex for granted. Ostrofsky reminds us that sex can become "like Diet Coke in the fridge. You know it's there whether you are thirsty or not."

HAVE *SEX* LIKE YOU JUST MET . . .

Ask your guy to say no to you sometimes. Have him play hard to get. See if that doesn't make you want it more.

Try to look out for moments when you normally wouldn't be thinking about sex—like when you're in the car on the way to his mom's house, or after an exhausting evening of house painting—and jump him. You'll not only remind yourself that sex doesn't have to be predictable, but you'll remind him too. An easy way to spice things up!

Ask your guy to keep things interesting by mixing it up for you on occasion. Ask him to plan date night every once in a while and see what he can come up with to surprise you once he's wooed you out of your clothes. But then make sure you reciprocate. "Yes, you know each other's signature moves over time," Ostrofsky says, "so that means committing even more to making it interesting."

It's Not You; It's Him

Okay, now imagine this scenario: Your guy pays more attention to his Blackberry than to your vagina. Most nights, he's the one to roll over and say he has a headache, while you're left in the no-nookie lurch.

Maybe it's stress that's getting to your guy. When he walks in the door, give him time to de-stress—and remember not to add to it by mentioning that the cat tore up the rug and that he forgot to pay the rent. Instead, table stressful discussions for later on, once he's decompressed. Offer to give him a nice, long back massage, complete with sensual oils. See where the massage takes both of you. Go hiking or running together—exercise goes a long way toward extinguishing stress and, as we mentioned before, strengthening libido.

Not stress-related? Examine what other things might be making your guy lack the sexual initiative. It's probably not you. Maybe you've turned him down too many times in the past, and he doesn't want to face rejection again. Say yes to sex when he initiates it—even if it isn't at what, to you, is the "perfect" time. Drop the sponge and step away from the sink; the dishes can wait. And remember that you should be the one to initiate the sex 50 percent of the time. We know that women like to be wooed. But put your Disney fairy-tale dreams aside and embrace your inner seductress.

Another explanation for your guy's lack of enthusiasm: Maybe he hasn't felt that he can please you in bed, especially if you're not reaching orgasm. Reassure your guy that sex is exciting and pleasurable even when you don't climax. Make it a positive experience. While you're having sex, be sure to make sounds that tell him you're enjoying yourself. We're not recommending that you lie or fake the big O. We're just suggesting that you make it known that you are enjoying yourself. Guys like positive feedback—make him feel like a sex god, and perhaps he'll want to get that feeling back . . . again and again.

Your guy might not say it, but he might not be getting what *he* wants in bed. Ask yourself if you are reciprocating. Do you expect oral sex but have no interest in giving a blow-job? Seriously, suck it up and blow your guy. (Sorry. There is no delicate way to put it.) It's really not that bad, right? If you are truly uncomfortable with oral sex, try cleaning your guy, down there, gently. Or, Valerie suggests, "Shower together first." Not only can the rub-a-dub-dub be a turn on, but perhaps once you have a clean, um, slate, you can try a south-of-the-border kiss and follow it up with a little lick. You do not have to start out of the gate with a Jenna Jameson deep throat. But making the effort shows him that you care about his pleasure too.

Be extra careful of your own negative behaviors in bed (review the Club Sexy manifesto!). Remember not to criticize or ridicule and to keep sex a positive experience. Steinhart suggests that you "say, 'I like it when you . . .' 'I love it when you . . .'"

If you have asked your man for more attention to your details, and you still aren't getting the overhaul you want, look for other distractions in his life that may be interfering with the sexiness.

"My ex could spend a lot of time ogling a marijuana bud, but when it came to the prospect of a roll in the hay, he was less than enthralled," says Nina.

If drugs, alcohol, or even video games have a grip on your guy's attention, there may not be much you can do. If you have confronted him and offered him suggestions to get a handle on his addictions, it really is up to him. All you can do is refocus your energy on yourself and away from enabling his unhealthy behaviors. We hate to say it, but if in the end you have to walk away, it is a lot better than relying on a partner whose attention is almost never available to you.

Of course, Ostrofsky points out, "You can't expect your partner to provide for every need but intimacy on all levels is a must. Hand-in-hand with that is communication: asking for what you want openly and getting the same in return." So if you haven't begun a dialogue yet, now is your chance.

Of course, if your guy is an extreme case, maybe he's having a medical problem that's keeping him from, well, getting it up.

According to Dr. Kilpatrick, "Sexual dysfunction can lead to personal distress and have similar effects on one's psyche as, say, depression." If all else has failed, he should seek help from a doctor.

We Asked. **He Answered:**

Q: *Why do you think a woman should be able to express to her guy what she wants in bed?*

A: I feel so much better being able to satisfy my partner to the fullest. I think it's important for women to know what turns them on and how to achieve the most pleasure. If a girl can "dirty-talk" her guy into getting her off, that's always best and it never makes a guy feel inadequate. Women should know that for most men, getting the girl off is their priority." —KYLE

When It's Both of You

Maybe you guys have slowed down because you're both busy with different things right now. If you trust your partner, there is no reason to start calling in the private investigators. In fact, the sexiest thing of all is to go find your own important matters to attend to and not call dramatic attention to what is lacking. If you both have gone to your separate corners for the time being and are feeling okay about it, then maybe it, in fact, *is* okay. Steinhart thinks it's important to remember that every couple is different. "The expectation can change. Are you both comfortable with no sex?"

Honestly, we're guessing the answer here is no. (The proof? You're reading this book.) If somewhere in the back of your mind you feel like there is another way to enrich a relationship you already like a whole bunch, you might be absolutely right. But there is no need to force anything, and you have our full permission to take it slow.

We have met and totally understand the phenomenon of romance-free honeys. We have two reminders for you. First, romance is a direct result of an unusual behavior. In other words, Natasha, a stay-at-home mom in Columbus, Ohio, says, "My husband is the least romantic guy on the planet. But sometimes I notice that he always comes home and helps with the kids without complaining, walks the dogs, takes care of things that I forget, and then rubs my feet at the end of hard days." The truth is, the lady with the eight dozen roses over there is probably thinking Natasha has the most romantic guy on the planet! So, look for "romance" in your man's mundane actions. You might be surprised.

Second, be romantic. Guys often aren't sure what we mean by romance and are afraid to attempt it and fail. Maybe the last time your guy bought a girl a white teddy bear and a rose for Valentine's Day she laughed in his face. We advise *you* to be the romantic one. Put a note on his lunch napkin or in his pocket. If you travel for work, always bring him home a present. Once in a while, have a bath drawn when he gets home from work and tell him to relax for a while until dinner's ready. Plan date nights and romantic getaways. Pretty soon, your guy will not only think he has the greatest lady in the history of the world, but he'll want you to know that he knows it. And if he still isn't getting the hint, end a romantic note with the simple words, "please write back."

Sometimes just stepping out of your real life can add just the right amount of adventure to your lives to reawaken the sexy in your twosome. This can be so exciting and romantic! Getting away from the stress of your real life—and putting your relationship somewhere else—can be just the thing you need to get back on track.

"B&Bs are great," says Sasha. "Even if it's just the next state, it feels like a romantic getaway, especially if there's a hot tub!"

Valerie is also a fan of hot tubs. "I went on a weekend trip with a guy I used to date," she says. "The room had a hot tub. We had such an amazing time just enjoying each other in that tub."

If money's an issue, consider doing an apartment swap for a weekend in a city within driving distance. Or even try to snag a house-sitting job that puts you in a different place, if only for a night.

Day trips can also be exciting, as can simply taking the time to do some activities together that don't involve pushing remote-control buttons or changing diapers.

"I like the idea of going for a walk or hike in a park and bringing food to have a picnic," says Amy. "Or, if you ski, going skiing and then hitting the lodge for hot cocoa. I don't think either of those cost much."

Take turns planning the date. Maybe plan one once a month. Take time and make the effort to make the date special for the other person. Sometimes feeling loved and wanted is as simple as knowing someone else really considered you and what you'd want to do for an evening. And feeling loved and wanted is very, very hot.

If you both feel comfortable, make your romantic rendezvous *about* sex.

"A friend told me about this book called *52 Invitations to Grrreat Sex*," says Tara. "It has fifty-two tear-out pages that fold into envelopes and have specific sexy scenarios on them. You take turns with your partner, leaving one for him as an invitation and making a date for sex. For some, you need to get props or wear certain things to prepare. Then you meet up for the 'date' and act out the scenario. My friend said that she and her husband had the most amazing time. There was talk of orgasms."

You could check out that book, or make your own sexy challenge and turn it into a game.

"Be sure to 'christen' every room in your home, one day at a time," suggests Sasha. "When you're done, start again with different positions."

We've got more ideas for games to add into your repertoire in the next chapter. What's important here is not only that you're getting it on, but that you're connecting, and, often, connecting means letting go of your inhibitions.

"Laugh, joke around, be silly," says Amy. "I think the levity makes everything less serious and then you can open up in general and have more fun in the bedroom."

Sexy Weekend Checklist
All the supplies you shouldn't forget to pack.

❑ Lingerie
❑ Massage oils
❑ "Do not disturb" sign
❑ Birth control
❑ Trail mix and energy bars (think of it as a marathon!)

- ❏ Red Bull (or maybe it's less marathon and more all-night rave)
- ❏ Toothbrush and toothpaste (We've already established that no one wants to make out with Morning Breath.)

We Asked. He Answered.

Q: *What is your best lesson you've learned about female anatomy?*

A: *Don't touch the vagina for about 10,000 years. Tease, get real close, blow cool air all over the place. Tease tease tease . . . forever. Then, tease some more. Even if the begging begins— and it will begin—do not touch. Then when you begin, very gently, you've basically gone three-fourths of the distance to her orgasm." —HENRY*

The Last First Kiss

To really get yourselves started "spicing things up," remind yourself why you fell in lust with your guy in the first place. "Sometimes it's as simple as starting over," suggests Vanessa. Mental images of your days as a young-and-in-love couple could be enough to conjure feelings of horniness. Start a conversation with him about the first time you kissed and the first time you had sex. Ask him to recount the things he was thinking, wondering, touching, and feeling. Bring the passion and mystery you're both visualizing into the bedroom with you.

"[The first time] was hot," says Rachel. "We waited a little while to have sex, so that built up a ton of sexual energy between the two of us. I think it is just a great feeling to not be able to get enough of each other sexually, and I love the beginning of a relationship because of that."

You might want to take it a step further and actually re-create the magic by re-enacting it. Go back to where it all began. Revisit restaurants, bridges, and even college campuses. If you met at a friend's wedding, go back to the venue. If you met when you were kids, revisit the old haunts and neighborhoods.

"We were once at our alma mater for a wedding, and we sneaked into the classroom where we'd met," says Tara. "We kissed there. It was really sweet—and felt a bit naughty."

Meet up with your guy as if it were a first date. It doesn't have to be like your actual first date—it could be more like a fantasy situation if you want. Ask "getting to know you questions" in new ways and see what you discover about your guy that you never knew before. And remember, you don't have to take it seriously the whole time. It's okay to laugh. It really is a little silly to pretend to be meeting someone with whom you share a toilet. Let yourself let loose. Let yourself be a little less familiar. Let him make sexual innuendos, or make them at him. Remember—flirt!

Relive your first kiss over and over, in the exact same spot—or in somewhere new and different. Picturesque places like a cliff overlooking the lake or on top of the tallest building in town are nice, but it could be anywhere, really.

"We were crossing the street, and I told my date—who became my boyfriend—that this was one of the best first dates I'd ever been on," says Rachel. "Then I turned bright red, but he said, 'You know what? I was thinking that too,' and then he grabbed me and kissed me. Then the traffic light changed and the guy behind us said, 'You can go now!'"

To make a repeat performance of your sweet and sexy first moments together, all you have to do is remember. To amp it up a little, use your imagination. Change your name. Change your character—you're not you but seductress Anastasia. Use an accent or a costume. Use tongues and then no tongues. Smooch against walls or in the middle of a busy sidewalk. It's fun and sexy.

Sasha sums it up: "When we were first dating, it was somewhat long-distance, so we only saw each other on weekends. Therefore, we were so built up we couldn't wait to attack each other—and did for the entire weekend. So as unsexy as it might sound, scheduling sex not only keeps it a priority, but the excitement leading up to it puts you in an amorous mood all day."

We don't want to suggest that one of you move to a different city or anything, but Sasha is on to something with this one. If sex and longing are just not up to standards, plan a vacation with some girlfriends, or go visit your sister for a long weekend. We understand the value of your vacation days and not wanting to use them up without your guy. However, going away without each other for a few days might be a great way to rekindle those old times when you longed for each other. If actually leaving town is impossible, plan a slumber party at a girlfriend's house. Or, if an overnight is out of the question, just spend an evening apart, each of you going out with your own friends. (Yes, hire a sitter.) When you come back together, we are pretty sure you'll want to hear all about your respective nights. We suggest you tell each other all about it, naked.

CHAPTER 8

TRYING NEW THINGS: *GAMES,* TOYS, LINGERIE, *AND* FANTASIES

> My boyfriend kept buying me fishnets—from full body suits to knee-high stockings. I kept buying sweet cotton nighties and some silky stuff. Finally, one day it hit me. He likes fishnets.
>
> —Simona

It's all Fun and Games Until Somebody Loses a Dildo

If you've implemented any of the suggestions we've given so far, you're on your way to spicing things up. But don't think you're done. Listen here, sister: If you're really going to do this right, you might have to shake things up even more.

"Surprise is so important in keeping a relationship alive," says Zvolerin of Adam & Eve. "For one couple, it could involve dressing up in costume and role-playing. For another, giving a sensuous massage could be enough to light that spark."

So, first, figure out what things you might be comfortable trying out—think toys, games, lingerie, and fantasies. Go surfing on a website like Adameve.com or Bootyparlor.com, and get a feel for what's out there. Take in all the ideas in this book. Visit a naughty shop like Babeland, which is female-focused and has locations in New York and Seattle, or Good Vibrations in San Francisco and Boston. Don't live on a coast? Look up stores around you that cater to a female sensibility—because those stores off the highway with the massive "*adult*" signs are not exactly beckoning us either.

Think about what types of experimentation appeals to you. Then, try to figure out what *he* might be okay with. "Everyone has a different comfort level," says Zvolerin. She suggests asking yourself, "Would it surprise him if I said I wanted to blindfold him? Wear a strap-on? Do it with the lights on?"

"Experimentation" by definition probably will mean you are introducing something new to the bedroom. Maybe it's a zany position or type of foreplay, a sexy bustier or even a toy. Sometimes when two people have a routine, something new can seem exciting—but it can also seem foreign, scary, or threatening. If you're afraid to broach the topic with your guy, easing your way into it is a good bet. Steinhart recommends a casual approach that suggests that maybe you didn't think of this out of your own sweet, innocent brain but rather that something else *made* you think of this. "Bring in a catalog—an Adam & Eve or Babeland catalog, for example—and say 'Look what I happened to find.'" Then flip through and see how he responds to the different products in its pages. Talk it out. Maybe you can decide together the types of things that would be worth a try and the types that aren't quite your bag.

Another suggestion? "Say you went to a party [or wandered into a shop] where there were lubes and a feather boa," says Steinhart. She recommends mentioning to him, "There was a long peacock feather and fur-lined handcuffs, and I was thinking some of those might be fun.'" Then, flipping your hair with a charming giggle, ask, "'What do you think?'"

"Peruse the Internet and find some photos of different things," says Renee. "Then either causally e-mail them to your guy or print them out and leave them on his pillow with a note that says, 'Any strike your fancy?'"

Sasha recommends expressing an interest in trying something new and then leaving the final choice in his hands. "Tell him to buy them," she says. Of course, then you've got to place trust in what he picks out—and we're not guaranteeing that it won't be cherry-flavored edible panties or some robotronic, spiky vibrator that you wouldn't put near yourself in full chain-mail armor, much less near your naked, defenseless vag.

We Asked. They Answered.

Q: How do you feel about sex toys? Is there ever a time and place for them?

A: HENRY: Yes. It's always great to see her use 'em. Always great to have 'em used on you. For more on this, see my chapter "How I learned to put things in my ass and enjoy life."

A: DAVID: No. The way I feel about sex toys is the same way I feel about exercise equipment. I have no doubt they are effective at what they do, but everything you need for both sex and exercise comes free with the human body. The purest experiences come from using, and learning how to use, what you've already been given.

The Stuff You Wear Just to Take Off

Lingerie is a good place to start when introducing new things into the bedroom. "Though the lingerie doesn't stay on too long, my guy always seems to get excited about it," says Renee. So what is it about overpriced lace and spandex that can be so enticing?

"Variety in your lingerie wardrobe will inspire new scenarios and fantasies and help stir up desire, even if the initial lust has started to fade," says lingerie expert Sarah Stark. "Lingerie lets you reinvent yourself. When women buy lingerie, they are usually thinking only about their physical appearance—how to boost this or show that—but it can transform more than just your look, but your outlook."

Yes, wearing something sexy can be advantageous to you. We all know that guys are usually interested in pretty underthings, but lingerie can also make women feel good about themselves. Just putting on that teddy and stockings may be a turn on to *you*. Yes, you can turn *yourself* on. Seriously.

"Even just thinking about lingerie, and therefore seduction, temptation, desire, or lust, keeps the flame alive," says Stark. "Empower yourself. Don't become a bitterly resigned, easily overlooked hausfrau in schlumpy old clothes. Wear things that show you care about yourself, and there will be a trickle-down effect. You might even walk down the street differently when you're in silky undies."

So you're confident, not so shy—you're not holding back. And you can bring that confidence and openness into the bedroom. Yes, you can use what you're wearing as a conduit to amazing sex.

Let it get you in a good mood, a sexy mood. Hell, let it get you feeling a little bit like someone else. "There's something for everyone—the vintage vixen pin-up look, the girl-next-door wholesome look," says Stark. If it makes you feel a little weird, think of it as exploring a certain side of your personality. It's not like you're changing who you are, you're just dressing the part to feel a little more like that vixen that you already have inside of you.

So, looking toward the "personality" you're planning on bringing out in the bedroom can be the first place you look for inspiration when choosing the kind of lingerie you want to purchase. If you're thinking cheeky Marilyn Monroe-esque sexy, go for something white and silky with a halter neckline. Stockings with garters could finish off the look. If you're more into the vampy look, a black corset with a red-mesh thong could work. What will make you feel good—and send the right message about what you want to happen in bed?

Really, there are no limits to your choices. "There are so many amazing variations of lingerie out there—silky slips, retro-style rompers and teddies, cute cotton gowns," says Stark. That's just to name a few.

Even though there are tons of options, finding something that translates perfectly to your bedroom might be pretty easy. It seems to be that way for Rachel—she finds that she can't go wrong with this two hard, fast rules. "See-through stuff is an automatic turn-on," says Rachel. "Pretty much anything from Victoria's Secret works."

But if you're new to the whole picking out naughty lacy things, you might want to ease yourself in slowly.

"You can always test the waters by starting with something subtle and working your way up," says Stark. "Get a style similar to something you already wear but in silk. The racier, lacier things can follow. Don't try to shock if you've always been a cotton panty-wearing pacifist. Let the seduction slowly unfold. Assume you have a lifetime of lingerie-wearing opportunities ahead."

Look for fabrics like silk, lace, and satin, and items with extra embellishment at the neckline, a sweet skirt or ribbon ties that emulate a corset. Details often determine whether something is sexy.

Think about why people buy lingerie in the first place. Why is wearing it sometimes better than just going naked? Well, because it gives the suggestion of sex, shows some skin—and still leaves something to the imagination, right?

Instead of going for the teeniest, tiniest bits of fabric you can find, pick the body part you love the most and decide to show just that off. You've been doing lots of Pilates and want to show off your killer core? Wear a pretty matching lace bra-and-panties set. Your abs will be on full display. If you went for the nipple pasties and crotchless G-string instead, that tummy may get lost in the shuffle.

"Suggest, rather than scream," says Stark. "Think about the balance between revealing and concealing."

Also, think about what your guy might be into. What's *his* favorite body part of yours? Stark says that if he's a "butt man," you might look at boyshorts. He's a "boob man?" A push-up bra or bustier that shows off that amazing cleavage. "Leg man?" Put your gams on display with stockings and a garter belt. Some high heels can finish off the long-legged look.

The next time you two are shopping for major appliances at a department store, wander into the intimates section. Ask him to point out what catches his eye and pay attention. What colors, fabrics, and silhouettes is he drawn to? Is there a particular "look" that seems to be a running theme? Maybe he likes the sweet, girl-next-door look or the subtle feel of a dominatrix. What about the glamorous slip-dress style?

You can either buy something right then and there, or surprise him later on with lingerie that you chose while inspired by his picks.

We know what you want to know now. What about that lingerie he buys you—especially the kind that you're not so crazy about? Do you have to wear the uncomfortable plastic thong he got you last Valentine's Day more than once? No, you don't. But you *can* use it to your advantage—and his. Use it as an indication of what he thinks of as sexy. Replicate its cut and shape by choosing something similar in a fabric that *won't* give you a rash. We're guessing you can find something you both can agree on.

Take other cues from your guy. Ever noticed that he was especially keen to rip off your clothes when you were dressed for clubbing? Try a lacy bra and underwear set with garters, knee-highs, and stilettos. If your guy seems turned on when you get home from work and are still in your suit and skirt from your day at the office, try a look that includes a black slip, reading glasses, red lipstick, and your hair pulled back into a severe bun.

Once you've chosen your skimpy skivvies, you'll need to figure out exactly how you want to reveal them. You don't want to put them on *in front* of him, but you pretty much can't go wrong with any other way you unwrap the goods.

"Think about building up the suspense," says Stark. "Creating that frisson. Feeling the anticipation as you slowly peel away layers of clothing. That's what lingerie is all about. Dim lights, candles, and wine help too."

Maybe you've got your lacies on beneath your street clothes, and you treat your guy to a sensuous strip-tease. Or you sneak into the bedroom, put them on and lie on the bed, waiting for him to find you.

"I usually pick a moment when he's not quite paying attention and change in the bathroom," says Frannie, a teacher in Raleigh, North Carolina. "Then, I step out and reveal. Usually his eyes seem like they're going to pop out of his head."

Despite the benefits of lingerie, some people are still intimidated by the prospect of wearing it. And that's okay. But there are plenty of reasons you may want to try to conquer your fear.

"There's no denying that lingerie has an effect on many men, which could make it seem cheesy, cliché, or objectifying and anti-feminist," says Stark. But remember that there isn't anything anti-feminist about wanting to make your partner happy. He does things to make you happy too right? Plus, remember what we said about lingerie being empowering? It can be, especially if *you* pick it out, *you* feel good wearing it, and you even get a little horny thinking about wearing it.

Remember that this decision is totally under your control—nix the cheesy or objectifying crap for the kind you feel comfortable in. "You don't have to wear a lace cut-out teddy, fishnets, and marabou slippers, unless you want to!" says Stark.

Then, there's the idea that maybe you think you don't have the right body type for wearing lingerie. Well, we think that's totally absurd, but hey, we sorta get it. We see Giselle and Heidi modeling these sexy skivvies, and sometimes we feel like we don't quite measure up either. But then we take a step back and realize that *any* woman can look good in lingerie.

"Lingerie lets you display or downplay whatever you want," says Stark. And she's totally right. You can cover up that appendix scar with a high-waisted garter belt and boost a sagging bosom with some push-up padding.

"I am not ashamed to admit that 90 percent of my lingerie could be classified as 'hardware,'" says Simona. "Those super hardcore girdles and slips with powerful sucking mechanisms are right up my alley—and they are still sexy if you get them in black rather than that sick-looking nude color, even while magically flattening back fat!"

"Wearing *something* is much less scary than the full-frontal all-out nakedness of wearing nothing at all," says Stark.

We Asked. **He Answered.**

Q: What do you like to see your woman wear in the bedroom?

A: KYLE: A see-through tank top and panty-shorts

A: DAVID: Cute panties—nothing fancy. Not sexy, lacy whatevers. Cute panties are best.

A: HENRY: Big boobs.

After all, your guy cares about *you*, wants to be with *you*, and even though Giselle probably looks hot to him, you do too. This isn't time to run and hide. It's time to show off your best assets and the most provocative sides of your personality.

"Trying to avoid having someone notice your body—keeping the lights off and your lover at arm's length—isn't exactly a recipe for romance," says Stark. "It's hard to attain true intimacy if you keep your distance. That's why there's intimate apparel."

Pillow Talk

"Having sex is like playing bridge. If you don't have a good partner, you'd better have a good hand."

—Woody Allen

Much, Much Better than Parcheesi

It's pretty easy to *say* that you'll try new things and that you'll be open-minded and adventurous during sex. But often it's much more difficult to actually make that happen. That's why adding some icebreakers—or sexy games—into your routine can get you both into the mood—get you to loosen up, ease tension, and start you on the path of thinking creatively sexually. Remember those late night, summer camp/school trip games of Truth or Dare before which you instructed all your friends to make sure you got dared to kiss Mikey Malone? How much easier is it to try something you're nervous about when it means not losing the game? It's all about stakes, people. Who doesn't want to win? Or better, who wants to lose?

"I like any game where there is a tease or a kind of buildup," says Amy. "To me that is so sexy, because then you finally get to the release and it feels so good and worth the wait."

Many of these games encourage you to explore each other and get you talking about sex in a healthy way. "Anything that gets couples communicating is a good thing!" says Zvolerin.

Sounds pretty damned good, huh? Well, we've got some ideas for you—ideas that can get the foreplay started off right.

"We played strip poker," says Laura. "It was slow and tantalizing."

There are two ways to play strip poker. The first is to play a typical five-card-draw-type of game (see *www.thepokertrainer.com* or *www.wikihow.com* for the rules to any version of poker you can think of), with you each betting a piece of clothing—or actions (and we ain't talking walking Fido, at least not *that* Fido)—to stay in the hand. The winner of the hand gets to keep all the clothes that were bet. It's like betting money, except cheaper. The problem with this method is that, in order to win, one person ends up with both people's clothes, and the other ends up with none at all. That can be hot, so give it a try, or try it this way: Play a few hands of poker—maybe this time it's stud. Each time someone loses the hand, he or she takes something off. And no one ever puts anything on.

Pretty much any board game or competition can be made into a "strip" version. We also like the idea of using Trivial Pursuit cards to give each other little quizzes. For each incorrect answer, a piece of clothing must go. We think this is a particularly good one because, man, some of those questions are impossible! You'll be down to nothing in no time—but still slower and sexier than your average change-into-pajamas strip down. See the box later in this chapter for other strip-game ideas.

Let's get back to Truth or Dare (but seriously, have we ever really left?). This time, it's the adult version. "I would definitely do truth or dare," says Amy. "I've kind of been dying to try it."

Yes, now that you are older, in a committed relationship, and more schooled in the ways of the world than you were as a teenager, this game can only improve. Take turns. If you choose "truth," he has to ask you a question and you must answer truthfully—questions can range from the sweet—"Which of my body parts do you like best?" to the, um, salty—"What does my cum taste like?" Now, if he chooses a "dare," you might tell him to do his best stripper dance for you or to put on a blindfold, have his hands tied and look for the jelly bean you have hidden somewhere on, in, or around your body. Then lie down and wait for him to find it. You can make up "truths" and "dares" in advance, writing them on slips of paper and pulling them from two hats. Or you can make them up off the cuff, getting kinkier and kinkier as the game goes on. Whatever you do, be creative!

If you're not so sure you can come up with inventive, sexy scenarios, you might want to try an adult-themed game that's been created just for couples like you who are looking to spice things up. Any store or website that carries sexy products should have plenty of options to choose from. Some are similar to Truth or Dare or strip poker, but they help you out by providing the questions and dares for you. So you don't find yourself in some nightmarish adolescent flashback crying, "I have no idea what the hell to dare you to do!"

"We tried the Kama Sutra board game," says Vanessa. "Let's just say, it was chock-full of ideas."

We've seen cards with tasks on them that you keep by the bed. The idea is that you have to do one of the "tasks" on the card every day—no matter where it leads. There are also books and calendars based on the same idea, not to mention a set of dice you can keep by the bed and roll. One die names a body part—lips, nipple, and neck—and the other states an action—lick, bite, tickle—indicating what you have to *do* to that part. The suspense of not knowing what those dice will say next can definitely add some excitement. And taking turns performing these acts slows the foreplay down. It also makes it fulfilling for both partners. "Naughty dice . . . are a great way to explore one another's boundaries and erogenous zones," says Zvolerin. She also recommends getting a little artistic with some adult finger paints on each other's naked bodies.

For those of you advanced gamers who are ready to take your play to the next level, we recommend trying a little role-playing. Think about what turns you both on, and make up a scenario that fits it. Maybe you get inspired by a romantic movie you saw. Dress up like Scarlett and Rhett, and after he tells you, "Frankly my dear, I don't give a damn," give him something to give a damn about. Or maybe he's always been eyeing your old cheerleading uniform and once said something like, "I would have never gotten to date a cheerleader when I was in high school." Well, pull out those dusty pom-poms and don that pleated skirt. Pretend you're the popular girl making out with the tuba player underneath the bleachers and that you're hoping not to get caught by the principal who's sitting right above you. Or pretend he's the principal!

"I tend to dress up in sexy underwear and get into a specific mood," says Holly. "We talk beforehand about what each of us would try. I never feel whorish or slutty because my partner doesn't make me feel that way."

Remember that role-playing, like dressing up in sexy lingerie, doesn't mean either of you wants to be with someone else. You still will get turned on by regular, old each other afterward. It just means you're exploring those other sides of your personalities, having fun, playing make-believe. Be sensitive to each other and the things that could hurt or make each other uncomfortable, and you'll be fine. If you have a problem, tell your partner afterward and decide together not to use the words or actions that were harmful.

The same goes for acting out porn. It can mean fantastic things for your sex life—as long as you're communicating and being respectful of each other's boundaries. We know we already told you all about watching porn and acting it out way back in Chapter 4, but we just wanted to reiterate it here because, well, it can also be considered a sex game. Not a bad idea to try.

"Anything to add to the excitement is fun and a change from the ordinary," says Sasha. "So why not try everything?"

Strip Games: Fun Stuff That Ends in Nudity

- **Strip Monopoly:** Every time you land on someone else's property, you can pay in money, clothing, or action. The higher the rent, the more the landlord can ask of you. In other words, you owe a sock for Pennsylvania Avenue with no houses or hotels. But you pretty much owe something involving flavored lube if you land on Boardwalk with a hotel on it.
- **Strip Checkers:** If you jump him, he takes something off—or you actually have to *jump* him.
- **Strip Clue:** Every time you go to the Billiard room or ask about Miss Scarlet, you have to remove an article of clothing. To make a final guess, you have to be naked.
- **Strip Chutes and Ladders** (after the kids are asleep of course): Something comes off for every chute—everything comes off if you hit the big one near the top.

What That Lockable Drawer in Your Nightstand Is For

Toy. A very innocent word for something that's not always quite so innocent. Toys aren't just props or items that you bring into the bedroom with you. They're things that physically enhance your pleasure. And that's a reason people love them. It's also a reason some people are a bit put off by them.

Sex toys are often associated with masturbation. But choose them—and use them—wisely, and they can make sex with your partner . . . well, let's say, they can kick it up a notch.

So, like every new thing you introduce into the bedroom, you need to start in the right place. Take this advice from Zvolerin: "Begin with toys that are nonthreatening—and nonphallic!—and can be enjoyed by both partners. Depending on one's partner's reaction, feel free to up the ante from there!"

Yes, it's wise not to bring in a giant dildo right from the get-go—you don't want your guy to feel threatened, inadequate, or replaceable. Step away from the plastic penises!

If you're looking for something both you and your guy can enjoy, we recommend—and believe we've already mentioned—a vibrating ring he can wear on his penis. While you're making love, it stimulates your clitoris and gives him some sexy vibrations, too. Plus, they can easily be purchased at your local drugstore.

Like the sound of that? "Pocket Rocket massagers are a great way to 'enhance' the experience by providing clitoral stimulation during sex." This small vibrator definitely doesn't substitute for a penis, but you—or he—can use it on your clit during foreplay or even while you're having sex.

"I think he was surprised—pleasantly surprised—at how good the buzzing of the vibrator felt to him as well," says Vanessa. "He went from, 'Well, I guess you won't be needing *me* anymore,' to 'Honey, where's the vibrator?' pretty quick."

"Cock rings can extend the lovemaking session and heighten sensation for men," Zvolerin contiues. "Some are textured or have vibrators attached to stimulate the female as well."

Remember that you don't necessarily need to use a toy on both yourself and your guy for you both to gain pleasure from it. "Men often get very turned on watching their partner using a vibrator—either during sex or alone," says Zvolerin.

Check out Natural Contours massagers: small and organically shaped, they aren't at all what you'd picture a vibrator to look like. We also hear that the Hitachi Magic Wand Massager is quite good. The damned thing looks like something your grandmother would use on her neck, but it actually packs some O-inducing power. (Gasp! That naughty grandma!) And, we've seen it sold at American Apparel, making it perfect if you're afraid to set foot in a roadside sex shop. Just check out the online reviews for this one—other women seem to love it.

"The other great thing about the massager-as-vibrator technique," says Simona, "is that your guy will think, 'Back rub!' and the next thing you know, everyone's happy!"

As you've started introducing toys into the bedroom, be sure to get your guy's feedback on how each item felt—and whether he'd like to incorporate them in the future. And tell him what you thought too. "Communication is key, and couples should be able to be honest about their likes and dislikes," says Zvolerin. Of course, you might want to leave out the fact that there's no way he could ever get you off like "The Seahorse" does. Be kind.

Also, pay attention to your own body and what works best for you, personally. "Many women differ on how they prefer to be stimulated," says Zvolerin. "Some only get off on clitoral—external—stimulation, while others prefer internal or G-spot stimulation. For them, the Rabbit or G-spot vibrators would be perfectly suited."

It's also a great idea to get advice from other women on sex toys they've used and liked. So find a trusted friend and ask. Check out the "Best Sellers" at Babeland.com. Read online reviews. Check out our box "We Tried It!"—we got some good feedback on a variety of products.

"Generally, a product receives good word of mouth and is improved upon over time," says Zvolerin. "For example, the Rabbit vibrator had been around for quite a while, and then it was mentioned on *Sex and the City*. Overnight, the Rabbit was sold out in stores and catalogs across the country. Same thing with G-spot vibrators. Women like to share what works. And, soon, the designs are improved upon with added bells and whistles."

Depending on how much you two enjoy sex toys, the sky's the limit as far as how much there is to explore. "There are sex toys available with so many bells and whistles, you'd need a detailed manual to figure them out," says Zvolerin. "There are vibrators now that plug into your computer. There are sex toys that have twenty-five or more controls that allow you to select vibration speed, thrusting depth, etc."

So you're warming up to the idea of trying out a sex toy but still aren't quite sure because the kids, Fido, or your lovely, sweet cleaning lady might find it? Well, remember that you can easily purchase a lock-box or find a piece of furniture that has a lockable drawer. Also, remember those items we mentioned that really don't look dirty. "The Natural Contours massager looks like a computer mouse or a pager. And a Pocket Rocket could be confused with something to be used on sore muscles."

Some people wonder whether or not the toy could get in the way rather than enhance your relationship with your guy. Well, Zvolerin eased our mind about that. "I don't know of anyone who could ever replace another person with a sex toy," she says. "There's something about that skin-on-skin contact and the scent of that other person that just can't be replicated. Instead of either/or, can't we have both?"

"We Tried It!"

These women share what sexy toys and products worked—and what didn't—for them.

LIKED IT

- *"The Rabbit would entirely replace men if it could cuddle and clean the gutters."* —RANDI
- *"Booty Parlor Vibrating panties are pretty much as wonderfully awesome as they sound. The vibrating mechanism fits in a little pocket in the crotch of the panties, which my boyfriend thinks are 'hot,' especially since they attach with two satin bows that are easily undone. And it is very quiet and has multiple speeds that are changed with a remote you can give to him—or hide from him, depending on your relationship to vibrators."* —VANESSA
- *"I tested the massage oil trio called Massage à Trois by Booty Parlor. We only tried one of the oils so far, but I'd imagine the results would be the same. I think massage is always a nice low-key, romantic way to get things started. Plus, who would turn down a free body massage?"* —AMY

- *"As far as toys go, the Bunny Pulsotron is my favorite! Multiple speeds and great clitoral stimulation—it gets me every time."* —RENEE
- *"I have a small Adam & Eve vibrator. It definitely works. It is small but the vibration is powerful!"* —RACHEL

Lukewarm

- *"The Booty Parlor Massage Candle is mostly nice. It's not at all a strong smell, and when you rub it on each other, it isn't hot. It feels good dripping, but it rubs in a little sticky."* —VANESSA
- *"I have some pink Booty Parlor bondage tape. I have wanted to use it lots of times, but so far no luck getting him to try it. I'm not sure if it's because it's bright pink—maybe the girliness is turning him off?"* —RENEE
- *"The Magic Massager by Adam & Eve was totally unthreatening to my boyfriend because it looks like a big back massager instead of a typical vibrator. The only problem is that, in our house, it is mostly used as a back massager."* —SIMONA

Hated It

- *"I tried a kit of lotions and lube, and the smell was way too girlie and strong—I actually wound up throwing most of it away because I couldn't handle the smell."* —RENEE
- *"At first, I thought I confused the Booty Parlor Don't Stop Massage Oil with the vag lube because it was so sticky and the directions describe it specifically as 'never sticky.' The directions lie. And the lube does not rinse off in the shower without three good soapings. I'm still not sure it's gone, and it's been a while since I used it if that says anything."* —NINA

Fantasizing about Things Other Than Shoes and Your Boss's Decapitation

Fantasy, according to *Merriam-Webster*, can mean anything from an imagined idea to the imagination unrestrained and extravagant. When we talk about a sexual fantasy, we're usually talking about a sexual activity or act that someone often thinks about trying. Or perhaps you'd never in a million years try it, but for whatever reason it turns you on to conjure it during masturbation or sexual activity. Now, maybe you've never tried one of your fantasies because you're afraid your partner might think it's weird or twisted. Or maybe you just haven't felt inclined to bring it up. Maybe you genuinely enjoy the thought but not the action. Or maybe you're curious—but deep-down afraid.

Fantasies could be anything from getting a little foot rub before sex to having a threesome with a same-sex partner. There are even some disturbing ones, like rape fantasies or you know, the whole R. Kelly peeing thing. Of course, what's disturbing to you—or your partner—may not be for other people.

So, the question here is, do you reveal your sexual fantasies to your partner and let him share as well? Or keep them to yourself?

Before you decide, ask yourself what you want to get out of sharing these deep-down secret thoughts. "What's the purpose?" asks Steinhart. "I'm not saying you shouldn't, but what's the goal?" If it's simply to get a load off your chest, maybe you should keep your lip zipped. Especially if it could hurt or offend your guy, or make him feel inadequate. In other words, a fantasy that begins, "My ex-boyfriend walks into this bar and sees me through a haze of cigarette smoke" is not only cruel, but also impossible, since smoking is now banned in most major cities' bars. But seriously, any fantasy in which he does not or cannot physically or otherwise play a part will not be a fun start to sharing fantasies—except maybe the girl-on-girl ones. We're going with he won't mind that he has to "sit out" that one as long as he can "watch."

However, if you have a fantasy that you think he might be into too—and it could add a fantastic alternative realm to your sex life—maybe you should say something.

"It might feel weird, because you're uncomfortable, but it's not," says Steinhart. "[By even beginning to talk about fantasies] you're figuring out ways of making it safe. You're testing the water."

The same goes for asking your guy about his fantasies. But make sure you really do want to know before you start probing him for all the gory details. "Sometimes people ask as a way of testing," says Steinhart. "'Is it really me that he loves? Is it really me that he wants to be with? Why would he want to be with me?' That same insecurity." If that's what you're getting at, forget it. It's really common for people to have fantasies that have nothing to do with their present sex life, and finding out your guy has one could make *you* feel inadequate. Even though you probably shouldn't be offended at all, make sure you really want to know before you ask. In other words, are you trying to see if he will stop you with a hearty "Gross!" as you are describing removing the clothes off of his sexy office assistant just before launching into a description of her giving him a fully excellent blow-job? Because if he doesn't, what happens then? Oh, and incidentally who wins that excellent game? We're wagering no one.

There are a number of ways to start the fantasy discussion. The first begins at a long table in the dining room of a Bavarian castle with you in some kind of corset with a visibly heaving bosom. Just kidding! One way is to be as informal as possible, the opposite of costumed and heaving. If you have a partner who's particularly verbal or has dropped the right hints, figuring out how to push his buttons might be pretty easy. Or, if, on the other hand, you have been able to convey what excites you to your partner, the "discussion" will feel more like a casual chat, like with Amy and her guy: "I have this thing about being tied up, not in a bondage way, just lightly restrained," she says. "I'd mentioned a couple times that I really like that, so without my knowing he went online and bought this under-bed 'restraint set' which is basically straps that go under your mattress and then have soft velcro wrist-and ankle-straps. He opened the box while I was eating breakfast and showed it to me. Let's just say we emerged from our room two hours later and I was giddy the rest of the day. But all it took was his little effort of listening to me and finding something he thought I would really like—and he liked it, too!"

If Amy's approach feels scary or too far out of character, then we'd like to dive back into the game bag. Yes, Miss Serious, we know there is more to life than game play, but we're not entirely sure what. Oh, and games just make the awkward silly and fun. By sharing your fantasies as a game, you are in a way distancing yourself from the fantasy. You are only sharing because you *have* to, not because you want to, so it's not your fault. It's the *game's* fault. It's your winning spirit's fault. So go ahead and say you like spankings, say it because you *have to*. And then close your eyes, take a deep breath, and . . .

One game idea involves sitting down together and making two lists. First, make a list of all the things you'd never do. Then, make a list of things you'd like to try. Have your guy do the same. Then, compare your lists. The things that appear on both of your "Like to try" column, well, we think you should try them. Anything on either of your "Would Never Do" lists is off the table.

Remember that if your guy reveals a fantasy to you—one that you don't like so much—you shouldn't act judgmental or rude. Sasha says, "No matter how out there it is, it takes a lot of courage to open up like that so you should keep any shock or disgust to yourself." She continues, "If it's someone you are serious about, and it rubs you the wrong way, you can just change the subject and accept that it's a fantasy, not reality."

Sasha makes an excellent point. Not to beat the hot secretary cliché into a bloody pulp (even though we'd all like to), if your guy throws out that he thinks the idea of a hot office assistant is a great fantasy, be careful that thoughts of his *actual* secretary don't fill your head and set you on edge. And *never*, under any circumstances, should you then fire back with something that might get him riled up, like "Yeah? I have the 'sleeping with your guy's best friend' fantasy. Top that, Buster!"

Instead, the minute something freaks you out, get more info. Try, "What if I was your secretary instead of your lady?" That should bring help table the insecurity, especially when he replies with, "Well, that's easy . . ." and plants a big one square on your lips.

"I guess because I'd never carry out most of my fantasies, I figure he won't either," says Vanessa.

That's a great way to soothe yourself if you begin to feel the green-eyed monster rearing its head. Think to yourself, "Would I really fuck my doctor? I mean, he's nice and all, but Dr. Rosenberg is at least seventy and his breath is a little rank, I'm not gonna lie." Even if his office bitch, sorry, secretary is hot shit, he probably sees her as the person who schedules his meetings. And even if he doesn't, *she* probably thinks of *him* as her sweaty boss. So, that should make you feel better if all else fails.

We Asked. They Answered.

Q: *Why do so many men have threesome fantasies?*

A: DAVID: Because what is better than having two women giving you and each other pleasure?

A: HENRY: Really? Are you really asking this question? Two words: Doppio fellatio. Hello . . . ?

A: KYLE: The more the merrier.

If a fantasy suggested by your guy is something you would never, ever do, don't let that force you to put the kibosh on the fantasy altogether. Maybe there is a compromise out there that you can live with. Remember, all fantasies are expendable, so even a little left of center is a great victory for a person wanting to try something that's way out in left field. So try a move that gives him a similar feeling without actually doing the part that makes you uncomfortable.

For example, your guy offers that he'd love to pee on you. (Since we already unveiled this one earlier, we may as well take it all the way!) You may think, "But what about the sheets? My mattress! What if some gets on the rug?" Or just like, "Gross!" But what if you try it in the shower? Maybe that is a bearable prospect. After all, it's the same tub that held four cases of Rolling Rock, your passed-out cousin, and your passed-out cousin's vomit last New Years Eve. Plus, there's Comet.

Zvolerin also mentions that threesomes are common fantasies. (Really? Huh. We never noticed . . .) If you're not really into having another person in the bedroom, find a toy that can act as a substitute. "Try anal beads, butt plugs, or accessories that make you feel like you're adding a third party to the bedroom," says Zvolerin. "Hey, it's a favorite fantasy of a lot of people!"

We Asked. They Answered.

Q: Would you want to try a threesome with a serious partner? Why or why not?

A: *DAVID: I think most men prefer to fantasize about doing it with a long-time girlfriend, but when confronted with the reality of it, would probably understand it would change the relationship for the worse.*

A: *HENRY: It's a very big deal to introduce someone else to the situation. Long-term, might not be the best idea. Dan Savage says you need to be together for at least four and one-half years before attempting such tomfoolery.*

A: *KYLE: It would be hard to have one with a serious partner because the chances of either one of you "crossing the line" would be too high. In bed, everything gets intense and you wouldn't want to make someone you love feel bad or misinterpret what your loved one is doing.*

Or you could *talk* about a threesome. Describe two girls and a guy getting it on. Or even more fun could be choosing a girl (or guy) together at a bar and talking about him or her. When you go home (just you and your guy), talking out what exactly you would be doing if that third party was in the bedroom with you two. If things start to make you uncomfortable, go ahead and toss in the line, "Then you decided she was an ugly whore, threw her out and decided you could only ever be happy with me, for ever and ever!" Because just like choosing not to try a fantasy, you are similarly allowed to end it whenever it loses its luster. That goes for both of you!

How to Feel Safe Trying Things Out

Have you ever gone to a party with your guy and made a deal before walking in the door that if one of you was ready to go, all he or she had to do was stretch and say, "I can't believe what a long day it's been!" Or perhaps you agreed upon a discreet back pat or eyebrow waggle (if you know what one is . . .). No matter your method for getting the team out the door, the premise was the same: All for one and one for all. It makes going to the party in the first place pressure free.

The same goes for trying out each other's fantasies. Imagine how much better you will feel about taking out the Kama Sutra board game if you know that it can just as easily get put away. One way to do this is by incorporating a safe word into your play time. Safe words are common in the world of bondage and discipline, where simply saying no might be misconstrued as part of the action. Typically, the word is designed to alert "the dominant" when he or she is approaching uncomfortable boundaries. Your word can be something silly that will take you both out of the mood, an inside joke that removes the drama and discomfort and reconnects the two of you. Any word, phrase, or idea is fine and can become a part of any new sexual behavior you and your guy want to try.

Say you are playing a game of Truth or Dare and suddenly you ask your man who he first jerked off to either in a magazine or in real life. Say his embarrassing answer is his step-sister and he doesn't want to talk about it. When he says, "Supercalifragilisticexpialidocious!" you calmly go, "So, baby. You hungry? I was thinking about popping some popcorn." Saying this instead of "No! Tell me who it is!" can only reap appreciation. And he'll be encouraged and comfortable to try other things with you in the future. The same goes for you too.

Renee says, "I would love to be blindfolded. There is something so exciting about not knowing what's going to happen but knowing it will be good because my guy always does things to make me happy."

It's a matter of trust. Frankly, if you haven't spent time cultivating a trusting environment outside the bedroom, it's going to be tough getting one started inside it. As we've been saying, figure out a way to feel confident in yourself and then spread that confidence into the way you treat your guy. Once you are there, you will be amazed by how far you can get in the bedroom.

It is easy to understand why. Sex is powerful. More than that, some fantasies are actually dangerous. We think that attempting a little bit of sadomasochism using hot candle wax is totally cool, but not with someone you don't trust to be totally careful with your velvety-soft complexion. The same goes for pretty much any exercise that puts your heart, sexuality, dignity, and flesh on the line. If you are going to try a little auto-erotic asphyxiation, for example, make sure you have as many safety precautions in place as possible. And do your homework! If he is the one who thinks choking you is a great idea, make sure you understand what is involved and plan a few escape routes. We aren't saying this to rain on your enhanced orgasm (as they say) but rather to remind you that INXS frontman Michael Hutchence will always be known as much for buying it with a belt around his neck in a hotel room as he will be for "Devil Inside." And there is nothing sexy about that.

Last but not least, we'd like to take a minute to remind you that even though most states have repealed all the sodomy laws, some things are still enforceably illegal. So, while we don't want to keep you from doing it in a dressing room, local park, or bar bathroom, if you get caught don't say we didn't warn you. Know the laws, and figure out the best ways to stay within them. Having sex in public places can include a friend's bathroom at a party. That's legal, even though it's a little rude. You can legally use a whip during sex as long as no one sustains an injury that can be presented as evidence of "assault" in a court of law. Again, we are not a legal book (we are very wise in many *other* ways), so if you and your partner are considering trying some BDSM (Bondage/Discipline/Sadomasochism), find out the laws, know your limits, and take the safe word very, very seriously. And for the sake of your parents who will have to hear the doctor explain what he removed from inside your rectum, make sure you trust your man completely and that he can trust you, because above all things, you are in this together (literally and otherwise).

Now go get 'em, Mata Hari!

CHAPTER 9

UTILIZING *TRICKS* OF THE *TRADE—* THE WORLD'S *OLDEST* TRADE

> The other day, my boyfriend and I were talking and the subject of past relationships came up, including some sexual things, and he said to me, 'You didn't do that, you're perfect.' He doesn't want to think of me in that [bad girl] light.
>
> —Valerie

Creating a Sexual Identity

A repair guy walks into an office after-hours. Only one executive remains finishing up some late-night details, so of course it falls to her to show the repair guy where the Xerox machine is. As a bobby pin falls out of her hair in slow motion and into the ample cleavage exposed by an opened button on her bursting blouse, the music comes on: Boom chicka wha whaaa . . . Boom chicka wha whaaa . . . etc. Is this the scene from a porno? Nope, it's one couple's Friday night date night.

As we stumble through our lives, our careers, and our relationships, it never hurts to gather as many tools, tricks, and weapons as possible for any hurdles we may have to surmount. In the workplace, one might turn to further education to learn the latest skills or consumer surveys to gauge public interest in your brand. At home you might upgrade to the latest technology in spray mops or window blinds. And in the bedroom, well, it might require everything from further education to the latest technology and everything in between. So, even if you have no intention of asking your man to meet you in your office after-hours dressed as a Fed Ex courier, one way to begin might be to break down why not.

In other words, what things about different scenarios turn you on? Begin thinking about what gets your juices flowing in order to begin understanding your sexual identity. "What is a sexual identity?" you ask. We'd like you to think of it as your naughty superhero alter ego. So if by day you are the mom who never misses a play date or the OCD neat freak who never misses a window streak, who are you in the deep dark of dirty (or just plain old) foreplay?

To begin, ask yourself what turns you on. We've been asking you for eight chapters now, so if you still don't have an answer, start simply. What attracts you to a man? If it's been too long to remember, ask yourself what attracts you to a movie character. (We accept answers like, "He was played by Taye Diggs," or "He looked really good in a purple Mohawk."). Valerie says, "I love it when a macho guy can be vulnerable." We don't want to tell Valerie who she is, but for the sake of discussion, let's say maybe Valerie has a little dominatrix in her. In other words, she might find it sexy to tame the wild. It is only the start of a larger dialogue we encourage you to have at least with yourself, if not with your lover.

Let's say, on the other hand, that you are more like Amy, who says, "I like a guy who teaches me things, like when Jordan Catalano taught Claire Danes how to drive a stick shift on *My So-Called Life*." Perhaps Amy is more submissive and likes having a lover who knows how to take control of a situation.

For Tanya, a grant writer in San Francisco, her sexual identity might already be more developed than she realizes. She already knows what activities are fun for her and her guy. "I think it's hot to include a little pain in a good sex session," she says, "especially when you are with someone you trust and you have a safe word to let the other person know when they've gone too far!"

Knowing your turn-ons is the first step toward recognizing a larger sexual identity—or alter ego. You do not need knee-length boots, invisible planes, or a cape (unless you want them), so don't worry if this identity develops slowly. It may be unlike any character you've ever met before.

The fact is, we understand roles and the rules surrounding them. As a manager at work, you probably know that it is a bad idea to smoke pot with your employees. As someone's sister, you probably get that you shouldn't necessarily discuss the Cartier earrings you got from your parents for your birthday when your sister got a candle from Kohl's. As a daughter, you understand that your parents may want the abridged version of your romantic trip to Vegas. And as an employee, maybe your boss doesn't need to see what you look like wasted and dancing on top of a desk at the holiday party. (So untag those Facebook photos, pronto!) We do well when we have boundaries and are able to fit into them. So while we are able to compartmentalize at work, with our parents and while on vacation, why wouldn't we benefit from setting a few rules for ourselves and the men we love in the bedroom?

We will not suggest that any of us are one or the other—in fact, we actually figure that many of us want to be dominated sometimes and want to dominate at other times. Sometimes we just want to kiss. Other times we want buttons to fly off in our blind passion. So, while you are unearthing who you are in the sack, who you want to be, and who you once were before it all went to the dogs—or kids—let us make it clear, this identity should be allowed to be malleable, it should be allowed to change direction at any time, and it should, above all things, include a safe word.

Superhero Sex

Want to discover your sexual identity? Use this cheat sheet.

We'd like to walk you through a few scenarios and break down what they are, to whom they might appeal, and how to bring them into your bedroom without finding your boyfriend sitting you down with a "honey, I'm worried about you" face. Why, you ask?

Well, for one, something might resonate for you that could help you and your partner to restart your proverbial fire. And two, it is very funny and interesting to read.

The Rebel Romance

Couples who found that being bad together felt so good:

- James Dean and Natalie Wood in *Rebel Without a Cause*
- Bonnie and Clyde
- Mickey and Mallory in *Natural Born Killers*

Guns a-blazing, the world's on fire, and they are both young and unlikely to get too much older. A union like this is probably made up of people who like adventure. By day, perhaps they play by the rules but wish they could bend them a little more often without losing their job during an economic downturn. Adrenaline keeps this pair hot and heavy.

If you can see yourself in this pairing or would love to, we recommend an afternoon of paintball or a good game of Grand Theft Auto (except when the dude gets in the car with the hooker—go ahead and act out what's happening in there). This is, of course, in lieu of bank robbery or selling drugs together, which are both a little hairier at the end of the day.

To keep the persona going over a long period, employ an ongoing game with twists and turns that will keep you both on your toes. Assign each other tasks (and we don't mean anything mundane like cleaning the gutters), such as finding buried treasure that you have hidden somewhere on your body . . . or have a standing date to get into character, pull out your (squirt) gun, and go looking for danger!

The Damsel in Distress and the Knight in Shining Armor

Couples who were turned on by a little lifesaving action:

- Cinderella and Prince Charming
- Snow White and Prince Charming
- The Little Mermaid and . . . well, you get the drift

The wind is whistling outside your castle window, and the trees are bending over as the sorcerer who kidnapped you in infancy from your royal parents builds the intensity of the storm. Your prince is climbing up to meet you and loses his grip in a strong gust. You gasp in horror! But being the stealthy dude that he is, he catches himself on the head of a gargoyle and continues to ascend. When he reaches the top, he doesn't even need a minute to catch his breath. He simply pulls you strongly into an embrace and kisses you. Hard.

There is nothing wrong with being a romantic by night and a career-driven über-bitch by day. We believe that a girl can have her whimsy and her whips too. If you are the kind of couple who wants to rescue and get rescued in bed, all the power to you! While some might view this as "traditional" and "ho-hum," we think that just because you found the dwarfs hotter than the prince doesn't mean you have to rain on other, taller parades. And anyway, being rescued is hardly par for the course. In our day-to-day lives we are all doing a pretty good job taking care of ourselves. Now that we aren't foraging for our food in the wilderness and relying on stallions to carry us around the forest, rescues are sort of a whole new perversion.

Damsel/Knight couples are likely to enjoy taking care of their partner, or conversely, enjoy being taken care of. You probably like it when your guy changes your oil, literally and otherwise. You probably enjoy it when he helps you climb over big rocks on wilderness hikes. You might even love burying your head in his very musky armpit during scary movies that you love going to see with him.

If you think it might be fun to see how getting rescued charges your batteries, we say, go into the unknown together. Allow yourself to act all girlie: Let the bugs be totally ick. Let the darkness be way scary. Let his arm protect you from the scary demons that await you, or the evil witches and their jealous wrath. Go camping together. Try hiking. If you really want to milk the genre, go to a Renaissance fair and dress in costume. Or if you don't want to leave the house, try a game of World of Warcraft or a Dungeons and Dragons session for two, both of which can be an ongoing source of excitement in your bedroom—as long as you actually, once in a while, get in bed!

The Teacher and the Naughty Student

Couples who make the grade acting out the lyrics to Van Halen's *Hot for Teacher*:

- Sting and Trudy Styler
- Indiana Jones and the girls in his archeology classes (See *Raiders of the Lost Ark* for details)
- Mary Kay Latourneau and the twelve-year-old boy who later became her husband

The senior class is finishing up their final. When you look up, you see that the class smart aleck is making a comment to the pretty girl in the third row, and she's laughing. You can't deny that part of the aggravation you feel is made up of sheer jealousy. When the bell rings, you ask him to stay. As the school empties out for summer vacation, the kid approaches your desk with that sheepish half grin you've come to like so well. You have him standing there, in front of you, ready to do anything you say. So, you let him . . .

This Teacher/Student identity is a classic and one that can be a whole lot of fun, no matter which role each person plays. In fact, we encourage this one be mixed and matched in a whole host of ways. This couple probably finds power incredibly sexy, since, as they say, that's what knowledge is. One person might be better at cooking and therefore is generally the dinner maker. The other person might excel at organization and is in charge of general housekeeping. Likely, this couple enjoys a division of labor, be it traditional or original, as well as a good lesson taught by the right teacher.

If this sounds like a blast to you, go out and do something at which each of you is a master. Make sure it is something you will like watching each other do. In other words, it isn't necessarily hot to watch your guy in a chocolate pie–eating contest and vice versa. We say, if he's a good driver, go to a racetrack and let him teach you what he knows. Is he a great painter? Have him show you a thing or two while you serve as his canvas. Are you an excellent Salsa dancer? Turn on some Celia Cruz and give him a taste of what you know.

Make the lessons an ongoing way to open your eyes to what makes each of you a great student or a great teacher, respectively. Like Lloyd Dobler teaching Diane Court how to drive her new car in *Say Anything*, sparks just might begin to fly. Just make sure you get to the good stuff before the bell rings!

Is Anal Sex the New Black?

There is a lot to be scared of when it comes to great sexual unknowns, so if this subheading is forcing you to read with your fingers half covering your eyes, we understand. We promise, this will not be painful, nor will it require you to bend over. All we are saying is, a lot of things that used to be completely taboo have now become, dare we say, nearly mainstream. But it wasn't so long ago that sodomy laws, or laws that prohibit any form of sexual behavior that does not lead to procreation, were still in place. In 2002, thirty-six states repealed these laws. A court hearing in 2003 invalidated the rest of the country's sodomy laws. Before then, giving a blow-job was, for all intents and purposes, illegal, as was anal sex and sex with vegetables.

Now-a-days, people, even *normal* people are seeking all kinds of sexual experiences.

"My ex-boyfriend and I were swingers for a while," says Tanya, "which was weird, because I'm from Kansas."

Tanya, it turns out, isn't all that weird. In the 1970s key parties became exceedingly common in suburbia. At these gatherings, car (or house) keys were drawn at the end of the night to decide who went home with whom. Now, swingers clubs are in every major city and can be found on many respectable Internet websites.

But is "swinging" right for you? It's really okay to say no to this question, not just about swinging but about any sexual behavior that makes you completely uncomfortable. In fact, it's rather important for the sake of your relationship that you know your limitations. Swinging, while totally right and healthy for some, can be horrible and depressing for those who just aren't into it. After all, it's one thing to accept your partner having great sex with a hot, buxom babe as long as you have your own superstar clone at your feet and are loving it. If however, you have the Gomer Pyle look-alike and your babe is with someone who resembles Pamela Lee, the story may have a different ending.

"One night a couple was coming on to me and not my boyfriend," says Tanya. "He started to feel really turned off by the whole thing. I was weirded out because swinging had always been his idea. Ultimately, we weren't able to find the right set of boundaries to make it work for both of us."

If you or your guy is interested in something out of the ordinary, it's okay—in fact maybe even better than okay—to have a look-see, which is different then a touch-see! In other words, look with your eyes, not your privates. If you are interested in swinging, for example, maybe start by reading about it online. The next step might involve going to (but not touching anything at) a swingers club. Go slowly from there, communicating with each other about how each of you feels as you go.

"I think it's okay to acknowledge the desire [to act out a fantasy], but also be clear about what bothers you about it," advises Amy. "Maybe there are more tame parts of it you can start with. Or you can come up with something similar that you're both more comfortable with. No matter what, I don't think you should do anything if you feel uncomfortable with any part of it. You may warm up to it down the line, but if you do and end up feeling cheap, gross, or used, that's unnecessary."

In other words, don't risk your heart on this, ladies. "A guy I dated used to ask me to 'stroke his cock,'" admits Rachel. "He used to tell me how hard and fast he liked it. At the time, I did it because I *thought* I liked it, but looking back, it was awful. It made me feel like I was being used . . . and I didn't get *any* pleasure out of it. Ugh."

If you are unhappy, grossed out, bored, or all of the above, it's okay to dial it back or stop the activity all together. Remember, sex is supposed to be fun—for both parties.

Know your limits, but don't be afraid to push them just a little, like Amy, who says, "I know my husband is curious about anal, to see how it feels, but I'm not into it at all. Sometimes I joke about letting him do it, but ultimately it grosses me out for poop-related reasons. I'm mostly into the 'lite' version of things, I like being tied up and spanked, but not hard. Anything I do, I leave pain out of it." If you or he are interested in trying something adventurous, baby steps are advised and encouraged.

Sasha says, "If your guy wants to try something far-fetched, I say go for it . . . you never know, you might like it. And if not, at least you tried. It's kinda like trying a new food. You know you love food—there are some that you don't, but you don't know unless you try them—it keeps life interesting, and the 'chef' will appreciate your openness and trust in him."

Holly, on the other hand, tried out her guy's desire and found it just didn't work for her. "He wanted me to tie him up, beat the shit out of him with a whip, talk down to him, and spit on him to degrade him," she says. "I tried but I couldn't stop laughing at how ridiculous I felt and how pathetic he looked. I get really turned off by a man who lets me walk all over him or who is needy."

We'd like to take this opportunity to encourage laughter, but only if it's not hostile or demeaning. But funny can be good, and surprisingly sexy.

"I had this pair of vibrating panties . . . Don't ask," begins Vanessa. "One day I put them on with a sexy bra and called my boyfriend into the room asking him if he could get something for me. When he walked in, I flipped on the vibrator, and holy shit! I couldn't stop laughing for fifteen minutes. But then the sex was great!"

The bottom line is, try to open your mind to new and interesting experiences but make sure your relationship is already built on a sturdy foundation of trust and respect. Then take it slow. And if you find you don't like something, stop. Your guy will understand and respect that choice if he loves you as you should be loved. And if he doesn't, heed this advice from Holly: "Find a new man who will appreciate you and make you feel like a sexual goddess."

Pillow
Talk

"Easy? You men have no idea what we're dealing with down there. Teeth placement, and jaw stress and suction, and gag reflex, and all the while bobbing up and down, moaning and trying to breathe through our noses? Easy? Honey, they don't call it a job for nothin'!"

—Samantha, *Sex and the City*

Turning Your Man from Vanilla to Super Sexy

So there you are, you and your beloved accountant. He is still wearing his tie and coat after a busy day at the office, and his hair is still cleanly parted on the left. Now, where do you begin the conversation about the crotchless panties you want him to get you for Christmas?

"I suggested using a vibrator, anal stuff, joining the mile-high club—mid-twenty-hour flight in the bathroom—you name it, and got turned down for everything," woefully confesses Sasha. "How did I ask?" she continues, "I just said, 'Hey, let's try . . .' I don't know. Maybe there's a better tactic that would've been more successful."

There is nothing certain about how your guy will react when you admit to him that you think the hottest thing you can imagine is for him to dress up as the Joker from *Batman* and spray (fake) acid on your skin. Yeah, that might freak him out, especially if he is a guy who likes his steak medium-well and his liquor on ice.

Holly says, "My partner and I are really open about sex and we discuss our desires. I try to bring it up in a light manner."

We like that technique, as long as you two aren't at your niece's hockey game and suddenly announce that you'd be interested in having him whip you with an Indiana Jones bull whip.

In other words, be appropriate. Maybe while you are tenderly kissing him on the neck and over his eyes, ask him in your best breathy vocal, "What do you want me to do to you?"

"Talking about what you want is often easier and better received if both people are sharing," says Nina. The truth is, you can also help demonstrate polite responses for sharing potentially embarrassing information.

Holly also suggests turning it into an everyday conversation. "Just talk about it," she says, "and come to a decision on whether or not you are willing to try it."

"But," continues Nina, "don't be afraid to laugh about it, because the suggestion of using a cucumber in place of a penis is funny, even if it does turn you on."

Share Nicely

Life coach Lauree Ostrofsky gives this advice about sharing your fantasies with your partner:

- "Think before you speak: Be honest with yourself about what you want and how he can give it to you.
- "Tell and show: Be clear in the words you use, and don't be afraid to lead him the first couple times.
- "Get him to share: It's likely he wants something too so open a dialogue in and out of the bedroom.
- "Be patient and proactive: You may not get it right the first time, so give yourselves a break. And keep at the creativity and communication."

Taking the Dirty Back

We've all heard those urban legends from our guy friends: The time that girl let him stick it to her from behind while she had her period—he left a bloody handprint on her wall. That scary dominatrix girl who didn't only reveal a sex swing but a nasty temper to boot and gave him that awful scar on his back. That girl who queefed about ten times while they were doing the Reverse

Native American Totem Position. It's enough to make any girl think, "Wow, if I try something new and kinky with him, will I forever be 'the girl who stuck her stiletto heel where the sun don't shine' behind closed locker room doors, between snickers?"

But think about "those girls." They were all one-night stands, flings, mercy fucks, and booty calls. Not one of them was a girlfriend, fiancée, wife, or "steady chick." They probably weren't even *ex*-girlfriends. We're pretty sure that guys don't talk about the women they've been serious about like that. Usually, when a guy badmouths a woman behind her back, it's because he never, ever, ever plans on seeing her again (well, except maybe for the occasional drunken blow-job)—but not because he didn't like her adventurous spirit.

That said, what if you've done something really, really naughty with your guy? And maybe you're a little embarrassed or not sure you want to do that again. You've opened Pandora's juicy sex box. Can you ever close it again?

Well, sure you can. Many couples can have kinky sex—and then have regular sex. And, if they feel like it, have the kinky sex again.

"Only one or two times did I feel sort of like an object, and I'm not really sure why," says Amy. "But we're good, so it wasn't something we had to bounce back from."

It might have been easy for Amy, but for others, the kinky sex gets a little out of hand, and something needs to happen to get things back on track. If this is the case, first open the lines of communication. Putting it in the back of both of your minds isn't going to solve anything.

"If a woman is uncomfortable or unhappy, I think she needs to be very honest, because this is about her and her body and self-esteem as much as it is about the relationship," says Amy. "She needs to look out for herself. So I think she needs to try to be as honest as possible about what is uncomfortable and why she thinks it might be."

"Try talking to him, introducing new things, making an effort," says Holly.

By new things, we're guessing she doesn't mean a new ball gag. Maybe it's massage oils or sweet romantic music. Maybe even a verbal affirmation that you still care about each other, even though your sex right now is more about fucking and less about wine and roses. A reminder that no one here's an object or a plaything can keep things from going from fun to shameful.

"Even during down-and-dirty sex we say, 'I love you,'" says Amy.

And it's okay to take a break from the down-and-dirty. Occasionally, make the effort to sweetly gaze into each other's eyes, play Marvin Gaye on the stereo, have the roses and the wine, and have "I love you" sex. Don't let romance completely die in favor of the kinky stuff.

So why, exactly, is "making love" so appealing?

"It brings you closer and is more intimate," says Sasha. "Hot and bothered is easy, but when you're actually able to be vulnerable and look in each other's eyes, it's more meaningful and more about love than animal instincts."

"It makes you feel beautiful, validated, and loved and like the sexiest, happiest people on Earth. And any insecurities melt away for a while. I like to have a good balance of this with the down-and-dirty," says Amy.

To Holly, it's the post-coital rewards that make cheesy "I love you" sex so great. "The way my partner looks at me afterward—I just get butterflies in my stomach," she says.

So remember, if the romance gets lost behind a wall of schoolgirl costumes and butt plugs, it might be time to reintroduce yourselves to each other. As in, "Hi. I'm Suzy, your girlfriend who loves you and wants to just get held sometimes and be called pretty and sweet and smart and not just, like, hot and very, very naughty . . ."

Make the effort and it will work. If not? "If the guy hears that and isn't accommodating or pressures you more, then you should get out," says Amy.

CHAPTER 10

KEEPING IT *HEALTHY* AND *FUN*

" I recently withheld sex to get him to get out of bed and get some DIY jobs done. I think it's an age-old truth that if the woman's not getting it on in her head due to emotional distractions, it's harder to get it on down below. I find that alcohol helps—and talking out your problems, of course. "

—Lucy

I'll See Your Two Weeks of Lawn Mowing and Raise You a Hand Job

Nunchucks, brass knuckles, the softball bat you still have from your days in the lassie league: These are all things that can be used as weapons—and should be, if say, Freddie Krueger finally escapes from your dreams and is standing at the foot of your bed. Sex, however, should *not* be. And really—even though he royally pisses you off sometimes—you shouldn't be using weapons on your guy anyhow, don't you think?

One way people often make this mistake is by letting sexual favors become a bargaining chip, a way of manipulating or coercing the other party to do something, as when you tell your guy he'll get some if he finally fixes that squeaky door.

"Using sex as a weapon is like using a scooter to drive cross-country. It's just not practical. Your best bet is to say exactly what you want, and trust that he will do it," says Ostrofsky.

In other words, as motivated as he might be by sex, it probably ain't gonna work in the long run. Men don't like to be manipulated, and they probably won't continue to allow it to happen.

"I try that almost daily—he just laughs at me," says Anna, a psychiatrist in Queens, New York. "I usually try to bargain with oral sex. He doesn't believe me and I rarely mean it."

We know it can be really difficult not to let life's other frustrations overlap into the realm of sexuality. For example, everyone has times that they're not in the mood because there's been an argument or disagreement. "I don't see avoiding it, since we are the same people when we're arguing and not thinking about sex, than when we are," says Vanessa.

Give yourself permission to be angry when you're angry. If he's trying to start some canoodling with you, and you're not up for it, go ahead and tell him that it's not the right time.

"Often when I'm grumpy, I don't like to be touched, or even hugged. I find it annoying," says Amy. "Obviously, when I'm really mad I don't want to have sex. For me, I usually just need a night's sleep to get over it."

Tara agrees: "I don't believe the whole 'never go to bed angry' thing," she says. "Sometimes you both just need to cool off and concentrate on dreamland for eight hours. My guy and I have done this. In the morning, you forget what you were mad about in the first place, or you realize you were being stupid. Then, you're ready for great morning sex."

But remember, not everything is worth holding on to for eight hours. Sometimes you should just let things go. It's not right to let your emotions totally take over and become a barricade between you and your sexual relationship. If you do that, frankly, your sex life could become obsolete.

"Sometimes we just get over small arguments, and sex after that is extra good," says Lorna, a graphic designer in Columbus, Ohio.

And we definitely don't recommend "angry sex." This guy is someone you care about, right? Then why would you take something that's supposed to be a loving act between the two of you— or maybe it's a grappling, raunchy sexy act—and make it about how mad you are right now? Plus, when your emotions are all out of whack, the sex might be really, really bad.

"If we've had an unresolved argument we both know that sex at that time is just not going to be good so we wait until we're both ready," says Lorna.

"Sex can make you feel a little better, but ultimately, if you're mad at each other, you have to talk it out," says Amy.

Ricki, a nonprofit manager in New York City, admits, "Oddly, [fights] often made things better . . . Make-up sex."

Okay, so getting over a fight is a little different than using sex as a weapon. It's okay to say you're not in the mood because you're upset about the fight you had earlier. But it's not okay to say you're not having sex with him until he changes the stinky kitty litter. Really, you're an intelligent, articulate woman. Do you really need to resort to using your body to get your way?

"That just feels wrong and sorta cheap," says Carrie.

Sex is not a reward, and it's not a punishment—it's something you and your guy *share* together.

In the heat of the argument, take a step back if you find yourself wanting to say something like, "Fine then! Have it your way—but that means no sex for a week!"

"Ask yourself, 'What are we fighting about right now?'" says Steinhart. "What is it that you want?"

The truth is, if you're so desperate as to bring sex into the equation, maybe there's something underlying that's really serious—and that's what you're *really* mad about.

"It's often something important, not just that he didn't take out the trash," says Steinhart. "So you're going to have to sit down with yourself and ask what are you really hurting over? And why would you want to hurt him so deeply?"

Sexual power plays can be irrevocably damaging to relationships. Withholding sex to feel more powerful can be a major indicator that you and your guy are creating some serious and unnecessary drama. Not to mention that it could be stifling or compromising to your partner.

"A friend of a friend had a boyfriend who refused to have sex with her often," says Tara. "People thought it was because she was beautiful and amazing, and he wanted to feel like he was the dominant one in the relationship."

And all the while, remember to keep your sex life sacred. Try to keep fights about dishes, kids, or pets out of the bedroom. Because they belong in the kitchen, playroom, and scratching post, respectively.

We Asked. He Answered.

Q: *Why do you think people end up together for life?*

A: Because true growth and evolution, spiritually and emotionally, requires a constant. And, regardless of your belief system, the best achievements in life shouldn't be experienced alone.—DAVID

Why Am I Not in the Mood?

There are other reasons people choose—or choose not—to have sex that are often considered unhealthy. Yes, we've already mentioned that it's perfectly okay to say no to sex when you truly aren't in the mood. And, of course, there are lots of great reasons to have sex. (Isn't that why we're all here?) But here's where we tell you to pay close attention to the reasons *why* you're either turning him down or starting him up, especially if it's becoming a monotonous pattern or your partner is pointing out the frequency.

Why ask why, you ask? Well, if you find yourself saying no a lot, or hearing your partner say no to you quite a bit, it could mean hurt feelings, ulterior motives, or a sign of a greater problem.

When you find that you're not in the mood, ask yourself why. There's a difference between saying no because you have a raging fever and saying no because you want to hear the latest Britney Spears gossip on *The Insider*. Or, as another example, if you have a report due for work, that's one thing, but if you *always* have a report due, that's something else entirely.

Remember when we talked about treating sex with your guy as a sort of haven or oasis? Well, this is just the sort of thing we mean. When we say don't bring work into the bedroom, we don't just mean papers, laptops, and Blackberries. When you're about to set foot into your haven, take a deep breath and let everything else go, perhaps *including* the once-in-a-while report that's due. Make a note to be in the moment with him. Smell his skin, look into his eyes, *really* feel every caress and touch. You need to let go of outside distractions and let the mood come over you. Life's stressful. We're all stressed. But letting stress interfere with your sex life, well, that's so not sexy.

Self-esteem could also be a factor in a low sex drive. Sometimes low self-esteem can inhibit people's libidos, in which case, maybe you or he—or both of you—should seek out a therapist. The other thing we need to point out is the manipulation that can go on here. Turning someone down to make yourself feel better in turn hurts them greatly. If someone is so willing to hurt the person they're supposed to care about, then there's a real problem and the relationship should be re-examined.

Lack of sex can often be a sign that there are other problems in the relationship that need to be resolved; if you feel this might be the case, we recommend you seek help from a professional.

Another harmful behavior is making your partner feel guilty for all the times you *don't* have sex, or when he won't do certain acts—for example, it's not a good idea to say, "Well, maybe if we did anal every now and then, I wouldn't play so much Wii on Friday nights." I know we're trying to promote lots of good sexual escapades with this book, but incessantly complaining about the nature, frequency, or quality of sex isn't going to change anything. Just like when you nag at him about using a glass instead of drinking straight from the milk carton, the more you harp, the less it's likely to happen. Instead, take some of the *actions* described in this book. And quit your complaining. However, if you want to open up an uncomplicated, un-manipulative dialogue with your man when you feel rejected by him, we salute you. In case you haven't figured it out, we are enormous fans of calm, rational, considerate communication. For example, if the two of you disagree on the frequency of sex, sit down and come to a compromise you can both agree on.

And remember, who ever heard of an oasis that contained bartering, bargaining, manipulating, or harping about sex? There is no such thing. In an oasis there are only palm trees, gentle breezes, blue water, and positive observations about the shapeliness of asses. Trust us. We know of what we speak.

Sex Gone Wrong

So far in the book we have spent a lot of time trying to guide you toward making choices that are both healthy and fun. However, sometimes things happen to a sexual relationship that cannot be solved by an oyster dinner and a quick game of strip poker. If one of the problems described in this section has reared its ugly head, you need to get help. The funny thing about help is that everyone involved must agree that help is needed. If your guy is pretty sure that there is nothing wrong with losing his job because he can't stop using the company computers to watch porn, then it might be time for you to make some big decisions for yourself: Namely, can you live like this if nothing changes? Or should you get out? We cannot make this decision for you—we can only point out to you that it needs making.

If you decide to stay in a relationship that is compromised by addiction or psychological problems, you might want to consider seeking help for yourself. Learn how to value your own life, and we hope in the process your relationship will grow too.

Madonna/Whore Complex

Sigmund Freud developed this concept for men, but we think it can work both ways. In brief it means that a person has a hard time viewing their partner as both sexual and pure. We are happy to announce that most of the women we asked about this topic say it does not in any way apply to their relationships. However a few people sheepishly admitted it had been or was something of a problem.

Lucy, for example, was asked if she ever saw her guy as a sweet, nice hubby and no longer as sexual, and she replied honestly, "This has happened to me. Still figuring out how to cope with it."

It can be difficult to get back to a place where you see your man as the "ay Chihuahua!" he once was especially if you feel like you are suddenly his mother or daughter or some other asexual character in each other's lives. Sometimes this stuff is a phase. Lucy concedes, "I'm putting it down to the pregnancy," since she is hormonal and pregnant.

Ricki had this surprising reaction: "I didn't really feel comfortable with my serious boyfriend seeing me as a vixen in bed," she says. "To be honest I tend to be a way bigger slut with strangers."

If you find this is a recurring theme in your romantic life, this could signal a bigger problem. However, sometimes it's just being with the right person.

"I had a boyfriend once who made me feel really slutty whenever I made noise in bed, so I found I got really shy," says Nina. "But the guy I'm with now loves it. The dirtier the better."

And since we are beating the idea of relationships as cyclical into the ground, we'd like to offer it up again here. Give yourself some time to figure out if what you are going through is a phase: Did you just have a baby? Get married? See if things go back to normal after the dust settles. If they don't, get professional help.

The Mommy Curse

What if you did just give birth and suddenly your guy looks at you and thinks, "But you are the mother of my child!"? The opposite can and does happen too. We'd like to say it all comes down to hormones and that crusted vomit in your hair, but plenty of couples are still 100 percent thrilled when Grandma comes to take the kids to the park, and they get it on the minute the door closes behind them.

If you guys have a bigger problem than the normal stressors of becoming parents, and it is bleeding uncontrollably into your sex life, you might be experiencing the "Mommy Curse."

"My friend's father cheated on his mother when she was pregnant, all three times," says Vanessa. "Apparently their sex life never went back to normal and they got a divorce. He and his second wife never had kids, and I think they have a great sex life."

Vanessa isn't sharing that story to scare you. But you should know what you are dealing with. If you or your guy doesn't get help for this situation, or even if you do and cannot reconcile it, you may need to call it quits. The last thing we want to do is break up a family, but if this is truly an unsolvable problem in your marriage (and we're talking after serious work in therapy and on your own) maybe the conflicted person should think twice about making babies in their next relationship.

On the other hand, it is possible to be Mommy *and* the sexual being you once were. Sheila, a writer in New York City, found that it was a bit challenging at the beginning:

Sex was painful after childbirth! We waited the recommended amount of time and were eager to get back to that area of our relationship. We were exhausted, but I didn't want to be one of those couples who completely forget about that part of life. I was shocked that it hurt, and that it continued to be uncomfortable for some time. At first I didn't say anything, and my husband could tell that something was wrong. Finally, I admitted that it hurt, and that we needed to go slow. That helped tremendously—just making sure we were on the same page. I told him I felt like a broken plate that had been glued back together—functional, but not the same! I'm also happy to report that I no longer feel that way.

Maybe using honest communication and being patient and persistent can get you there too.

Addiction

We are going to address two types of addiction in this section: Porn and sex. The two, as you can imagine, are similar and often go hand in hand. We'd like to take a minute and say in no uncertain terms: *If your guy looks at porn on occasion, it does not make him a sex addict!* Ehem. Sorry for the outburst.

We've enlisted the help of a great expert on this one. Dr. Altobelli, who, as we've mentioned earlier, is an addiction psychiatrist, says addiction is a result of "engaging in a behavior that satisfies a need." The same neurotransmitters that are responsible for falling in love—dopamine, serotonin, and norepinephrine—are similar to those that are triggered during addictive behaviors like gambling and drug abuse. She calls the trio "the reward system of the brain."

She continues explaining sex addiction, saying, "It's progressive. The behavior becomes more risky and the addict will continue to do it despite negative consequences." In other words, sex addicts might continue the behavior compulsively even if they contract an STD, lose their job, or screw up their relationship.

So, it's important for you to take inventory of negative behaviors in your or your partner's sex lives and figure out how damaging they are to your love life as a couple. If you are just annoyed by porn, maybe you can give your guy a break and let him enjoy it once in a while. But if you are feeling like he almost always chooses it over real-people sex, try asking him to lay off it and on you for a while. If that doesn't work, it might be time to get help.

According to Dr. Altobelli, the object of the addiction "becomes less gratifying to the addict because it's never enough. It becomes as much about the obsession as the act itself."

The good news is, that is often why addicts decide they need to quit. But also like with any addicts, *they* need to decide. Even Dr. Phil, as we've seen, can't decide for them. Of course, staying quit is tough too. But it's possible.

"It can be treated the same way as OCD with high doses of serotonin reuptake inhibitors like Prozac and Paxil, as well as with family or couples therapy."

Now, let us say here that Dr. Altobelli is not *your* psychiatrist nor your man's, so if some of the info we just gave you about sex addiction rings true for you or him, the responsible thing to do is to seek help. This book, while we hope proves helpful, is not a doctor, nor does it play one on TV.

The Love Drug

According to Dr. Abiltobelli, "a serotonin reuptake inhibitor" is a drug that prevents your brain from allowing serotonin to simply "puddle" in your brain instead of cycling through or "reuptaking" into your system. When you are feeling really happy, like when you are falling in love or doing copious amounts of cocaine, your brain does not reabsorb serotonin effectively, making you feel elated and like you can do anything. That is, until you realize the guy talks with his mouth open, or ten minutes after the cocaine cycles through your body. Then it usually just sucks.

Fixing Things

So, let's say something has happened. Maybe you had a sex addiction but you got help. Perhaps your man cheated on you, but he recognizes his mistake and wants to try again. How can you fix something that has gone wrong?

"Unless you have the kind of open relationship where you can enjoy the cuddly bear, secure qualities of your hubby at home and eat out for your sexual needs, you're going to need to be able to get sex in-house, which may mean working at it," points out Lucy.

We agree that any long-term relationship requires long-term effort.

Anna suggests, "Talk, couples therapy occasionally, vacations away from life stressors, even small overnight ones, talk and listen!" to keep the relationship fresh and healthy. But if you are struggling through a betrayal or an indiscretion, yours or his—it's important that any decision you make for yourselves is based on you two and your experience. In other words, have you both acknowledged there is a problem? Are you both willing to work on the problem?

"If the person is an alcoholic," says Dr. Altobelli, "and you've said, 'You drink too much!' it's a pretty bad sign if the person replies, 'No I don't. You don't drink enough.'"

Our first tip for deciding to work on a wounded relationship is this: Do you both agree the relationship is wounded? If one of you thinks sleeping with the hottie during the overnight work conference in Buffalo is inevitable, and the other doesn't, you're not going to get very far in overcoming the hurdle. If on the other hand, everyone agrees that watching a gangbang on video *every time* you have sex (and we're going with more than once a year) being a little suspect, then we think there's hope.

Second, and this is totally about the two of you and how well you know each other: Do you think you can ever find trust in your relationship again? If you just aren't sure, and you believe you have really tried, we support a decision to move on.

But any time a relationship hits a bump, be it an ant hill or a mountain, be careful of jumping ship. We live in a throwaway culture. We'd hate for you to mistake a beautiful relationship for a replaceable toaster oven. See if you can fix it first, but commit to fixing it before moving on. We know it isn't easy. As Ricki points out after we asked her how couples could stick it out for the long haul, "God. If I knew the answer to that . . . ."

Don't worry. We'll get to that. It's our grand finale.

CHAPTER 11

THE *LONG HAUL*

" I think feeling and being physically close usually relates to being emotionally close, especially in a long-term relationship where you've committed yourself to a specific person. Also, when you really love someone, you want to make them happy and feel good, and for them to make you feel good. I know I like pleasing my husband and when he is satisfied, I feel happy. He feels the same way when I am satisfied. Even though you definitely get something out of it too, I think there's something really nice about trying to do that for your partner. "

—Amy

Fluctuating Trajectories and Other, Smaller Words

If a long-term relationship were a state, it would be Colorado, not Kansas. Forget flat, even, plain. If you're with a guy for years on end, there will inevitably be hills, valleys, rocky terrain—you know, stuff that Jeeps were made for.

There will be days when you're over the moon in bliss, thanking your lucky stars that you've put clubbing and Internet dating behind you. There will be others when you tear your hair out because he doesn't know how to unload a dishwasher; where you're completely bored and your eyes are wandering; when you're thinking about breastfeeding and getting that promotion more than you're thinking about your guy naked, not to mention remembering to think of him fully clothed. And sometimes days become weeks or months, maybe even years.

This isn't necessarily a bad thing, especially when the good outweighs the bad. You just need to be prepared that it very well could happen, and to stop yourself from concluding that the relationship is doomed just because it's happening.

"Is your expectation that it will be always be exactly like it was in your first few years?" asks Steinhart. "Or can you visualize that you grow together and then you grow apart and then maybe there is something that brings you back together? You might grow apart again, but that doesn't mean no one cares—it means you are getting on with your lives—you know, children or career—and then something happens and you come back together. You look at each other and you are suddenly present with each other again."

That doesn't sound so bad, does it? Actually, it sounds pretty damned romantic.

So naturally, your sex life could follow the same fluctuating trajectory.

"Sex is not its own entity—it's part of everything else that's going on," says Lorna. "Work concerns, family issues, and illness can all affect sexual relationships. There are hills and valleys, just like in the rest of life."

Yes, you may have dry spells.

"The busier we are, the harder it is to find the time [for sex]," says Carrie. "Sometimes the sex just isn't that important at the time. It is more about the relationship than the sex."

If you find yourselves rolling over and drifting to dreamland more often than ravaging each other, that could be totally okay. What's important is that you really ask yourselves if it's okay.

Steinhart points out that "there are other things that bind people in a relationship." However, there's a difference between "both people are happy" and "both people are happy *enough*."

For example, Jill, a casting director in Los Angeles, puts it like this: "I married a warm bear. He does not *ever* do unexpected things. He only eats honey, and sleeps and watches TV. If there is any attempt from my side to seduce him in any way, then, he goes to watch TV or eat honey. The only thing that stands between me and my libido is a sofa, a TV, and the bear's never-ending back pain." If it sounds like Jill made a bad choice in men, then read on. She continues, "But, in the game of mating, I know I won when I look at my husband. I usually know the whereabouts of my bear, and I pretty much know what is on his mind. And he loves me and *our* Baby Bear with all of his heart."

"Everybody is different," says Steinhart. "Are they comfortable with no sex? Are they masturbating at all? Or, are they thinking about it every once in a while?"

"It isn't always just that it's missing. It can be that it's missing—and you miss it," she continues.

If the status quo isn't okay, with you—or him—100 percent of the time, you're going to have to change it up. You'll have to find a way to end those dry spells, to find each other between the sheets, and to make sure that you also have times that you look at yourself in the bathroom mirror, hair tousled and crotch sore, smile and say, "When it rains, it pours!"

Is There Any Truth to "The Seven-Year Itch"?

We asked women what they thought of the theory that after seven years of marriage, people are prone to stray. (The term is best known from 1952 Marilyn Monroe flick by the same name.)

"I do think there is some validity to the seven-year itch. For me, I think it has more to do with curiosity, since I've never been with anyone else. And it's looking only! I think mostly it comes out of the need to have attention and be desired in the same way your partner did in the beginning." —AMY

"Nay! People make shit up to rationalize. For some, fidelity is harder." —ANNA

"I'm sometimes inclined to believe in the seven-year itch based on other people's relationships. Generally, those I know who injected a new dynamic into the relationship before the seven-year

mark—they got married, had a baby, or moved countries—made it through. Those who just kept going as normal tended not to make the cut." —LUCY

"*I don't believe it for a second. Sure, some people have extramarital affairs. Some don't. People get tempted. People resist. You can't put a timeline on how long you can stay faithful for. And if you do, you're bound to fail at long-term monogamy.*" —TARA

"*I think there is a seven-year itch for everything.*" —RICKI

There's No "I" in Team

So, with all those ups and downs, how do you make your relationship work in the long run? How do you keep yourself and your guy happy and satisfied? How do you remember that he's the one and only person you want to be with—and not that cute construction worker who whistles at you every time you wear a skirt to work?

Well first, remind yourself why you're in this relationship in the first place. "If it is worth it and you cannot even think of living without the person, then you have no choice but stick it out," says Carrie.

Can't put your finger on exactly why you can't live without him? Hell, make a pro and con list—whatever you have to do to get to the reasons he's the one for you. "One of the best parts of being in a long-term relationship is having that tacit partnership, someone who's on your side, knows you inside out, has the same ideals, norms, and values," says Lucy.

Keep your attitude toward him and your relationship positive. Keep your words, thoughts, and actions in check.

"I still think being silly and laughing together is one of the most important things," says Amy. "And you really have to like and respect who you're with."

Remember that he's your partner, not your punching bag, not your child, not your enemy. Treat him with the love and respect you expect him to have for you. Nurture your partnership. Show him that he's truly your teammate in this battle that is life.

"You have to respect your man and have him be a partner for handling little things like household chores, and big things like important financial and family decisions," says Amy.

"I think everyone wants to feel as though they are part of a team when it comes to relationships," says Rachel. "You want to feel as though you have constant support and someone who understands you and is there for you through thick and thin."

"At one of my favorite weddings," says Ricki, "the bride and groom high-fived like two teammates who just scored a goal— or touchdown, basket, or whatever—and it was the cutest thing ever."

Committing to another person, be it over fish sticks in your living room or during a ceremony in front of 250 of your closest family and friends, is about becoming a team. And together it is about scoring life's goals and weathering life's losses. That's the big picture. If you have concerns or grievances, or you're upset in any way, find the proper way to talk it out and then do it.

"Don't let irritations build up," says Lucy. "The worst thing that can happen is that indifference takes over from anger or frustration. That's the point of no return."

"If you feel that he dominates and doesn't give you a voice, or you feel like you have the whole burden on you, you will feel taken for granted and probably become bitter or feel undervalued," says Amy, "and that will not help a relationship last, certainly not happily anyway."

Also, don't freak out about the changes that are likely to occur along the way. "Some people become desperate," says Steinhart. "They think, 'Oh my god, he's changing! That means he doesn't love me . . . he's going to want a divorce.' Abandonment issues come up. Have some confidence in the long term."

Trust your partner. And trust yourself. Sure, your eyes will wander. You'll think that guy in line at Whole Foods asking you about your local organic turnips is hot. Your heart may even go pitter-patter. But you can walk away from him without acting on your impulse, never to see him again and know that it was okay that you got all giddy and flirty for a second there. You're a strong, confident, sexy woman. You don't need to sleep with other people to *feel* sexy. But sometimes it's nice to receive the occasional "How *you* doin'" and bat your eyes with a flip of your hair and big toothy smile.

You'll also need to make it a point to actually *use* the ideas and tips you've read in this book. "You know each other's signature moves so over time you'll need to commit even more to making it interesting," says Ostrofsky.

And how exactly do you do that? "You have to work at it," says Amy.

Playing the Part

So, maybe now you are convinced that you'd like to have a relationship that is among other things, sexual. You could just live with him as a buddy, but as Ricki points out, "Why not just live with women, who are, let's be honest, generally more interesting, better cooks, and less smelly?"

So, if you are cultivating a sexual relationship, have a little respect for what each of you considers sexy. This does not mean you need to starve yourself or get your hair bleached.

"If you want to be viewed like a vixen, act like one!" says Lorna. "This means not wearing your old college T-shirt and flannel jammy bottoms to bed. And no flossing in bed!"

Anna says, "I can see the possibility that, if people don't take care to stay healthy or fit as they age, they'll become less attractive." She also says, "I think it's easier for women to feel sexy if their men think they are."

But finding yourself attractive is often the first step. That means if you have a few extra lumps and bumps, learn to love them or take the time to lose them.

Also, put yourself out there in the bedroom a little more. Maybe you are still a little nervous about the time he asked you if he could rain-check sex one night, and you took it to mean for several months. It's not any one person's duty to initiate sex. So, if you want it, go get it. Trust us, once you get going, you will forget how the whole thing started.

The longer you are together, the easier it is to fall into routines. "It's Tuesday," you think. "This is the night I do the two-minute blow-job, he does the two-minute going-down thing then he gets on top, four thrusts, I finish myself off, bathroom, and bed." Worse still is when you are so comfortable that wearing a green face-mask, changing your tampon, and shitting in front of him have all become par for the course.

"My mother had the best birth control," says Lorna. "After she had her hair done each night—teased and sprayed into oblivion—she would wrap it in toilet paper and put on a hairnet before going to bed. Can't imagine my father could find a vixen through all of that."

Even if it hasn't gotten that bad, a little effort to close the bathroom door and to wear some silk undergarments never hurt anyone, did it?

Sexual Healing and Feeling

It's not like we haven't mentioned that it's important to connect sexually in your relationship. But here's where we hit the point home.

Sex is something that only the two of you share—and it might be the only thing that's that exclusive "in any part of your life." It's what you have together that bonds you, that helps you find each other at the end of the day, that lets you escape from life's stresses and pressures and know in that instant that you are with the one with whom you are in love.

"Sex is the greatest form of intimacy," says Lorna.

It's important because, as Lucy puts it, "Otherwise he is no different than a best mate."

"Having that desire there keeps things exciting and interesting," says Amy.

And Anna points out that physical needs are essential to happiness. "Human touch makes people kinder and softer," she says.

Let's face it, it's not just the actual act of having sex that's good for you, it's *feeling* sexy too.

"Feeling as though you are sexual brings a sense of confidence to your life and makes you feel desirable, which is important no matter who you are!" says Rachel.

Lucy says it helps with "self-esteem, keeping your zest for life and stopping you from feeling old or worrying that the best days of your life are over."

Ostrofsky agrees. "Your physical needs are just as important as your emotional and intellectual ones and deserve the same kind of nurturing to keep you happy," she says.

And hey, don't forget about *him*. You love him, and you want him to be happy, right? Well, we're guessing he'll be a lot happier when he's getting some good lovin'.

HAVE **SEX** LIKE YOU **JUST** MET . . .

"It is also vital to see your partner as a sexual being too, as sex is such an important part of a relationship," says Rachel. "It brings two people closer together and allows you to feel intimacy, which is so important."

As we mentioned before, people who are happy in their sex lives tend to be happier in their relationships. All those endorphins that are released during sex make you happy. Feeling intimate and close with your partner makes you happy. Feeling like being with him in your oasis makes you happy. Seeing him sexually can make you happier with him as a partner, too.

"Otherwise you just have a male roommate who leaves the top off the milk and pees on the toilet," says Amy.

And, really, don't you want to be happy?

Why Does Sex Matter?
These women sound off.

"It just does." —LORNA

"Apart from the overwhelming amount of research that highlights all the medical and psychological benefits of regular sex, it's a basic carnal need for the majority of us." —LUCY

"Everyone needs it. If you aren't going to get it in the relationship you are in, then you will look somewhere else." —CARRIE

"To me being married and choosing to only be with one person is an intimate gift. Aside from the emotional aspects, sex feels good physically and releases chemicals that make you feel good and happy. It's an extra boost that can keep interest high." —AMY

"Sex brings people closer together!" —RACHEL

"Well, primarily 'cause it makes babies and secondarily 'cause it is fun."
—RICKI

The Physiology of Love

Long-term relationships are worth having and worth keeping sexy.
We think that is a safe thing to say. According to Dr. Altobelli,
"Dopamine is responsible for the giddiness of falling in love. It's
why people get OCD about each other." Why you can't get him out
of your head. "That feeling is what the whole dating industry is
based on!" she says. What she means is that we can't help wanting
new love. We are addicted to it.

"But it is endorphins that keep long-term relationships going,"
she continues. As when you jog, that burst of happiness that eventually becomes quiet contentment is what will help your long-term
relationship increase in strength and value. But you need to keep
jogging. No, we don't mean literally. We mean have sex! Because
endorphins are released during sex. Of course you also need the
romance, the intimacy, and also the surprises. (Good ones like love
notes, not bad ones like "I forgot to mention I got a job in Vancou-
ver. We move next Tuesday.")

It doesn't mean you don't ever get to have the dopamine kind
of love with your guy again. It just means that you don't get it as
often. And that's okay. Most of us would take long-term contentment over short-term OCD any day.

But you need to continue to release those endorphins, and sex
is one great way to do it. So, if you are coming from a place where

sex just hasn't been all that sexy lately, it might be due in part to a lack of sex. A catch-22? A little bit. But one that's fairly easy to get out of. And all it takes is a little effort from each of you.

Remember oxytocin, the chemical released in the brain during orgasm? (It's also released during breastfeeding—but hopefully that's not at the same time.) That's what usually makes it harder for women to "fuck like men," because we fall in love during our orgasms (and with our babies in a *different* way when we breast-feed). We think that's a lucky thing. We like it that sex makes us bond to our guys.

Making sex a priority in your relationship can mean excellent payoffs. As Steinhart points out, "It's worth it to build a great life. It's worth it to build a great relationship."

There is so much to a healthy, fabulous long-term love affair. As Ricki puts it, "I love old married couples. They just look like each other's best friends and teammates."

"Hard work is what makes a long-term relationship viable," suggests Nina. "Sex is what makes it enjoyable."

At the end of the day relationships are built on friendship, trust, mutual support, and a faith that no matter how many times you cycle apart, you will cycle back together. And then there's the sex. Don't forget about sex!

"Sexuality is icing on the cake!" says Steinhart.

Now, we can only hope that what flickered through your mind was, "Which body part is where I should spread the icing?"

Why not? It's your relationship. Go ahead and indulge!

RESOURCES

Experts:

Malee Ackerman, Interior Designer, San Francisco

Eva Altobelli, MD, Addiction Psychiatrist, New York City

Charles Kilpatrick, MD, Assistant Professor, Obstetrics and Gynecology, University of Texas at Houston, LBJ Hospital

Lauree Ostrofsky, life coach, Grounded in Potential, New York City, *www.groundedinpotential.com*

Judith Steinhart, EdD, health and sexuality consultant, New York City, *www.judithsteinhart.com, www.heyjud.com*

Books:

Apsan, Rebecca and Sarah Stark. *The Lingerie Handbook.* (New York, Workman Publishing, 2006).

Bass, Ellen and Laura Davis. *The Courage to Heal,* 4th Edition. (New York, Collins Living, 2008).

Cohn, Laura. *52 Invitations to Grrreat Sex.* (Oklahoma City, Park Avenue Publishers, 1999).

Davis, Laura. *The Courage to Heal Workbook.* (New York, Collins Living, 1990).

Harper, Dawn. *Sex Deck: Playful Positions to Spice Up Your Love.* (San Francisco, Chronicle Books, 2006).

Linder, Joselin. *The Purity Test.* (New York, St. Martin's, 2009).

Linder, Joselin and Elena Donovan Mauer. *The Good Girl's Guide to Living in Sin: The New Rules for Moving In with Your Man.* (Avon, MA: Adams Media, 2008).

Lingerie/Movies/Products:

Adam & Eve: Adameve.com, Adamevestores.com

American Apparel, Americanapparel.net

Babeland, Babeland.com

Booty Parlor, Bootyparlor.com

Candida Royalle, producer and director, Femme Productions, Candidaroyalle.com

Condom Country, Condom.com

Durex, Durex.com, Drugstore.com

Good Vibrations, Goodvibes.com

Natural Contours, Natural-contours.com

Victoria's Secret, Victoriassecret.com

INDEX

ABOUT THE AUTHORS

Joselin Linder and Elena Donovan Mauer maintain that they're "good girls" despite writing about things like vibrating panties and living, unmarried, with a guy. This book is a follow-up to their first title: *The Good Girl's Guide to Living in Sin: The New Rules for Moving In With Your Man*. Their popular blog on cohabitation can be found at *www.thegoodgirlsguidetolivinginsin.com*.

Linder is a writer and filmmaker. She wrote *The Purity Test: Your Filth and Depravity Cheerfully Exposed in 2,000 Nosy Questions*, an entertainment book of questions inspired by the online phenomenon. She wrote *The Ultimate College Prank Book* under the name "Mae B. Expelled." Her book, co-written with Gabe Zichermann, *Game Based Marketing* comes out in March 2010. She is a founding member of the Stoned Crow Writers Workshop, a fiction group that has carried on a weekly meeting since 2005. She lives in Brooklyn, New York, with her boyfriend, Aaron, who taught her that long-term relationships only get better with age.

Mauer is a writer and editor specializing in relationships, sex, health, and well-being. Her work has also appeared in publications such as *Self*, *Modern Bride*, *Bridal Guide*, and *Psychology Today*. She's been married to her husband, Anthony, since 2003 and lives in New Jersey.